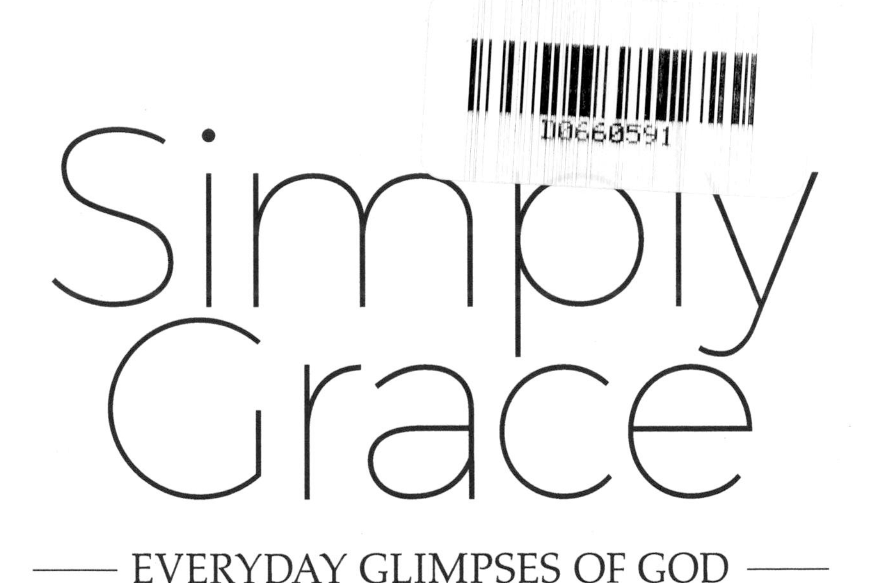

Simply Grace

EVERYDAY GLIMPSES OF GOD

BRUCE L. BLUMER

Simply show grace,

FB

Simply Grace: Everyday Glimpses of God

The General Board of Higher Education and Ministry leads and serves The United Methodist Church in the recruitment, preparation, nurture, education, and support of Christian leaders—lay and clergy—for the work of making disciples of Jesus Christ for the transformation of the world. The General Board of Higher Education and Ministry of The United Methodist Church serves as an advocate for the intellectual life of the church. The Board's mission embodies the Wesleyan tradition of commitment to the education of laypersons and ordained persons by providing access to higher education for all persons.

The Wesley's Foundery Books is an imprint of the General Board of Higher Education and Ministry, The United Methodist Church, and named for the abandoned foundery that early followers of John Wesley transformed, which became the cradle of London's Methodist movement.

Simply Grace: Everyday Glimpses of God

All profits from this book will be used to support scholarships and building an addition to a school in LaGonave, Haiti, through the nonprofit organization LaGonave Alive. For more information see www.LaGonaveAlive.com.

All web addresses were correct and operational at the time of publication.

ISBN 978-1-945935-38-1

19 20 21 22 23 24 25 26 27 28—10 9 8 7 6 5 4 3 2 1

Manufactured in the United States of America

To the Blumer family, in honor of our parents, Boyd and Evelyn Blumer, and for extended family members' commitment to the United Methodist Church, including family members who have attended, served, and been employed by United Methodist churches, United Methodist–related universities, and United Methodist–related organizations.

Special thanks to my wife, Sharon, and my father, Boyd, for their editing and grace-filled suggestions. Thanks also to Rev. Kip Roozen for encouraging me to write a book on grace.

Contents

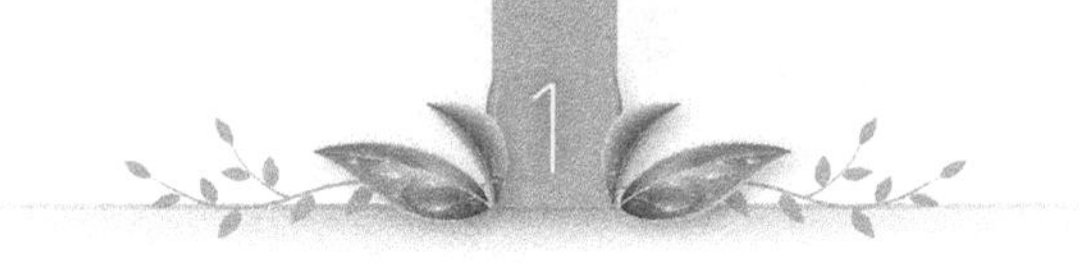

Everyday Glimpses of God

For though we may not live a holy life, we live a world alive with holy moments. We need only take the time to bring these moments into the light.

—Kent Nerburn, *Small Graces: The Quiet Gifts of Everyday Life*

At first, I thought it was children running down the stairs. Then the rumble made me think it must be a train, but I had never seen trains in Haiti. Then I knew. It was an earthquake.

I was serving with a medical team in January 2010 on the island of La Gonave, which is located just off the mainland coast of Haiti, about fifty miles from the epicenter of the massive earthquake. That night and over the next few days, we continued to feel aftershocks and uncertainty.

Because La Gonave is rural, there was relatively little damage to buildings and few injuries. We actually didn't learn for a day or two about the devastation that had taken place in the capital of Port-au-Prince and other places in Haiti. Unfortunately, our families bore much of the pain as they were watching horrific images on news media. We were unable to communicate with them that we were fine. In Haiti, when people find out about a death, there is a bellowing cry. We heard too many such cries over the following days.

Approximately three days after the earthquake, our clinic began to receive patients from the mainland who were injured and unable to find care. It is amazing, because to get to La Gonave it is an hour vehicle trip north of Port-au-Prince, then an hour or more boat ride through the bay, followed by a bumpy thirty- to forty-minute trip up a hill to our clinic. Somehow, they found us. Suffering from terrible lacerations and burns, one woman with a broken hip arrived, along with several others with broken bones. This was too much trauma for our little mobile clinic to treat. We sent word that we were closing our clinic, then hauled all our medicine and supplies to the only hospital on the island. And we waited.

My son went to the nearest ministry, about twenty minutes away, to send email messages to our loved ones back in the States. We were not in any immediate danger. We had food and water, but it remained unclear how we were going to get home. There was a flat roof jutting off our clinic building that provided a good view of the bay across to the mainland of Haiti. From that vantage point we could see boats and planes arriving, which we later learned were providing relief assistance. One morning as I was sitting on this flat roof I could feel the prayers. I have no other way to describe it—I had a palpable sense that people were praying for me, for us. From that time I have not doubted prayer. I am not completely sure how prayer works, but I know that God intervenes in our lives, and prayer is a path to that intervention. It was comforting in the midst of uncertainty.

God intervenes in our lives, and prayer is a path to that intervention.

As I was cleaning out emails on my home computer about a year after the earthquake, I found a folder that my wife had created, containing the many messages about our team being in the earthquake. So many concerned people shared ideas on how to get us back home, and countless indicated they were praying for us. I broke into tears as I read these messages. I was so humbled. It was also affirming. I realized that, as I felt those prayers on the roof, I'd encountered the amazing grace of God. It made me more aware of the ways God connects to our lives.

Another glimpse of God came through a Bible study I have been attending, made up of a great group of men who have met early on Monday mornings for about three years. This past year we completed our spiritual autobiographies, an introspective look at our lives. We reflected on the influences of our individual stories, including the people and life experiences that have impacted our walk with Christ. After spending several weeks working on our autobiographies, we shared them with the rest of the small group. One of the shocking realizations for me was that fully 80 percent of the group indicated that their dads either had died already or, in a variety of ways, were dysfunctional. This revelation blew me away.

Both of my parents have been incredible influences in my life. Not to mitigate the important role mothers play in our development and formation, but my dad has been and continues to be such a strong influence, role model, and support in my life. I rely on him for perspective, advice, and help in my spiritual journey. How I treat others is heavily influenced by my father. Unfortunately, having such an example, a father who serves as a spiritual model, is not a reality for many of the men in this group.

Being in the men's group also has helped me realize that we rarely know all that's going on in other people's lives. Here were guys with whom I'd spent three years meeting with regularly, in a group that did a lot of sharing, and yet I wasn't aware of the major events that had shaped their lives. We don't always know who among us has received a difficult medical diagnosis, who has lost a close friend or is struggling with a hidden addiction. We simply need to show grace to all those we encounter.

Within this men's group, in all our differences I've found one common theme—our life experiences have pushed us steadily toward God. Not by way of lightning bolts or burning bushes, not by easy or initially positive experiences, but we've each experienced nudges toward God that came through the right person at the right time and included circumstances that guided us on the right path, provided perspective, and offered glimpses of God's grace in our everyday lives. Through these and other experiences, from the insignificant to the dramatic, we began to see God. Through our common and ordinary lives, we discovered together that God's grace is present and freely available if we remain open.

So what is grace, and how can we become more aware and open to where God is leading us? Grace is simply the love God has for us. Grace is God's gift; we can't earn it. Grace is available to us regardless of what we've done or how we've lived. It's so simple yet complex. It's available, unexplainable, undeserved love. If we accept that we are loved, cannot earn grace, and have already been forgiven, it changes our relationship with God. We move to a new level of awareness, and in doing so we have the opportunity to change our lives dramatically for the better.

Grace is simply the love God has for us. Grace is God's gift; we can't earn it. It is available to us regardless of what we've done or how we've lived.

I was explaining to my father and favorite theologian, Rev. Dr. Boyd Blumer, that I was trying to make grace more understandable, to take away all the churchy words and make the concept of grace more accessible. He said this: "When we try to describe our experience of life and faith, our words are inadequate. So we use big words to describe concepts. It's also our temptation to tell others that *our* experience should be someone else's experience."

This book is my attempt to make grace understandable, to take fancy theological words and translate them into everyday words that anyone can understand. My hope is to explore with you the concept of grace and make it easier to recognize in our lives. Through stories and our collective understanding, we'll walk into grace together. Along this path, my prayer is that we discover God as God works in and through others and through our everyday experiences, to nudge us and, sometimes, seemingly shove us into being more as God intends us to be. It's simply grace.

We start by accepting that grace is unmerited. We can't earn it nor can we pay it back. It's truly a gift for which we simply need to open the door to receive. After we wrestle with the realization that grace is freely available, then we need to prepare ourselves to hear God. We need to become more mindful that God does want to intercede, but first we need to realize how grace might happen.

The purpose of this book is to make grace easier to recognize in our lives.

In his book *All of Grace*, Charles Spurgeon opens with the story of a minister calling at the home of a poor woman. The minister knocks at the door, and when no one answers he concludes that no one is home. After a while, he sees the same poor woman at church. The pastor indicates he visited her home and knocked several times but received no answer. "At what hour did you call, sir?" she asks him. "It was about noon," replies the pastor. "Oh, dear," she says, "I heard you and I'm sorry I didn't answer, but I thought it was the man calling for the rent." Spurgeon goes on to explain that grace is "free, gratis, for nothing." While we may feel God has expectations when God comes calling and that we have nothing to give in return, Spurgeon goes on to explain that grace is more like someone coming in God's name to *bring you* a free gift. It's meant to be your present and give you eternal joy. Through that gift God is saying, "Please open the door and let me into your life. Come now and let us reason together" (Spurgeon 1974).

For what can be known about God is plain to them, because God has shown it to them. Ever since the creation of the world his eternal power and divine nature, invisible though they are, have been understood and seen through the things he has made. So they are without excuse.

Romans 1:19-20, NRSV

Let's begin to discover God and find the seemingly hidden ways of grace. Grace is a simple and yet profound mystery of God's qualities, power, and nature. We can become more aware of how God might reveal those qualities to us through a beautiful sunrise, in a bird's song, in the wind through the trees, or in the crashing of waves. When we are aware and attuned to God, we can find God in a phone call or note from a friend, in hearing a song that brings a tear, in a phrase from a book, in an often-read scripture verse, or in sharing laughter with a child.

A few years ago I spent a weekend at a monastery for a personal retreat. It is the monks' custom to seldom speak throughout their days, even during meals. My time among them helped me focus on words and silence and other ways that God speaks. While there I spent time writing and reflecting on scripture, including the Psalms. Psalm 19 spoke especially to me. The first part of Psalm 19 tells us that creation itself pours forth praise for God. The heavens "pour forth speech" and "declare knowledge" of the Creator. That speaking and declaring comes without sound.

The heavens are telling the glory of God;
and the firmament proclaims his handiwork.

Day to day pours forth speech,
and night to night declares knowledge.
There is no speech, nor are there words;
their voice is not heard;
yet their voice goes out through all the earth,
and their words to the end of the world.
Psalm 19:1-4, NRSV

We tend to fill the silence with our words and busyness. Give us patience to listen for the still small voice. Let us be still long enough to become aware of Christ's knowledge. Let us be quiet enough not to miss God's communication.

Start looking for God all around you.

I encourage you to spend some time today without words, contemplating God's creation. Start collecting stories and examples of ways God and others seem to be prodding you to begin your own spiritual autobiography. Start looking for glimpses of God all around you. Be fully aware that God wants to be in a more significant relationship with us, that God's grace is fully open and available to all; and may God bring us into recognition of God's simple, yet amazing grace.

Let us pray:

Allow us a glimpse into grace, O God.
Let it sink in that there is nothing to repay,
That you'll be there in good times and hard times.
Let us learn from our everyday lives.

Let us find acceptance for your grace
To understand how simple yet complex
Are the ways you intersect and guide our lives
To be more like you each and every day. Amen.

Simply Grace Story: "A New Thing" by Rick

My dad and I haven't always had the best relationship. He encountered some difficult situations in his life that led him to be distant, and he eased some of his aches with alcohol. About a year ago, my dad started having some pain and discomfort. This pain continued for the next couple of months, and every time I spoke with him on the phone I could just tell that the cancer was getting worse. I sensed he was scared and worried; he wasn't doing his normal activities, working out in his shop on his cars, or even leaving the house.

I remember praying that God would make him feel better in an instant and that soon he'd get back to normal. As my regular calls to my dad continued, he sounded worse and more depressed. During one late Sunday afternoon phone call, Dad didn't want to talk. He sounded so down, so defeated. After hanging up with him, I whipped my phone across the room and I cried. I felt so disappointed! Why wasn't God doing anything?

Soon after, a worship service was held one night at my church—a time for prayer, singing, and community. During the service the pastor asked the group in attendance if anyone had prayer requests. I knew it wasn't going to be easy, but I felt that I needed to lift up my dad. The group gathered around me, placed their hands on me, and together we prayed for him. Initially it was awkward, but ultimately it was amazingly powerful to sense and know that people cared about me and my dad.

The next night I was at home, listening to a sermon online. The pastor was talking about the Israelites who were going through some hard times—trials and tribulations. The Israelites were worried and scared, but they were reminded of all the miracles and times that God had provided.

Do not remember the former things, or consider the things of old. I am about to do a new thing; now it springs forth, do you not perceive it? I will make a way in the wilderness and rivers in the desert.

Isaiah 43:18-19, NRSV

In the book of Isaiah, God tells the Israelites to forget about the things of old, stating, "I'm doing a *new thing*." This is exactly what I'd needed to hear. I'd been waiting for God to perform the miracle, to perform the healing he's done for people in the past. In the midst of this, I was missing the miracles already in progress.

Since that night, I've begun to realize that when God starts to talk into your life, you might not immediately see a change in your situation. Sometimes, it might first produce a change in you and *that* might be the new thing.

I've seen so many such changes in the past few months, changes that demonstrate how our God turns barriers into blessings. God is showing me all the new things, such as:

- opportunities to say "I love you" to my dad when we end our conversations (that's been a new thing);
- one-on-one conversations on trips to and from doctor appointments (that's a new thing);
- the proud look in his eyes when he's with his grandkids (the look isn't new but my noticing it—that's a new thing);
- the number of people praying for him, people he has never even met (wow—that's a new thing);
- opportunities to read Bible verses to Dad (another new thing);
- the demonstration of love that 450-plus people showed my dad at his cancer benefit— display of love and appreciation for a human life that few ever get to see;
- my mom's grace. My parents have been divorced since I was in middle school, yet she baked and bid on auction items so that her grandkids had something meaningful from that night, and all her siblings showed up for the benefit. Amazing grace.

I wish I could report that my dad is feeling better. Unfortunately, he's not. His cancer has progressed. But the awesome news is God is constantly doing a new thing *in us*. As we walk in God's way, we can trust God's will—even while we feel lost in the wilderness.

To be clear, I'm still praying for the old things. I'm still waiting for that Red Sea to part, praying that my dad will wake up tomorrow and feel no pain, that he'll be cancer-free. I believe and know God can do that. But even if Dad doesn't get better, I trust that the next thing is going to be the best thing. God has already moved so many mountains throughout my life, throughout my dad's life, that I know God is going to continue to bless us. But I don't always need to know how. God makes a way.*

Conclusion

God's grace is at work within us and within others. Sometimes God works through tough situations and old hurts. It might be a change within us, so we can be more aware of God and others, or it might be a slow change in the patterns and interactions of others. But without a doubt, God's grace is at work. Thank you, God, for grace and for continuing to bring new things.

Reflection Questions

1. Share an experience when you felt God's presence.
2. What new thing might God have in mind for you now?
3. Write a list of the ways God offers grace to you.
4. How would you explain grace to someone who didn't know God?
5. Where might you need grace in your life?
6. Keep a list of the ways God is showing you grace and how you might extend grace to others.
7. What do you take away from Rick's story?

*Rick's dad left this earth and started a new thing on February 8, 2018.

Grace Is Like That

"May grace and peace be yours in abundance in the knowledge of God and of Jesus our Lord."
2 Peter 1:2, NRSV

For those of us who don't think God has a sense of humor or don't think he teaches us, we aren't paying attention. Years ago, I was driving on Highway 18 on the Rosebud Reservation. I came over a ridge and saw something along the side of the road; it looked like a person but was moving strangely. As I got closer, I realized it was a man with a cane who was walking with great difficulty. He basically bobbed back and forth from leg to leg. It was very cold and windy, and he was hitchhiking.

So, while approaching this man on the road, I began to play the game of "why I can't pick you up." I'd been traveling and my car seats were filled with stuff. I didn't know this person. His legs looked stiff—maybe he had a prosthetic leg. Could he even get in my car? I'd had a bit of a scary experience once with a hitchhiker when I was in high school. Surely there would be other cars behind me on this lonely, desolate, freezing-cold stretch of highway in the middle of nowhere. And so, I drove on.

My destination was Mission, South Dakota. I was asked to serve on a panel that was being hosted on the reservation to get community members to organize and plan for their own future. My role was to talk about foundations and fundraising issues. Over a cup of coffee, I met with the coordinator and we talked about his expectations for me and for this project. We talked about the tough issues of isolation, prejudice in our communities and in our churches, and trying *not* to make this just another plan that led to another false hope.

About an hour later a woman appeared at the door of the ministry with a man—a cold, hungry man who had a very distinctive walk. The same man I'd left at the side of the road. A man who ended up in the very same place that I ended up. Then God showed me how people are meant to be treated, through the example of the directors of that ministry. They simply did what they always do—they fed this man, gave him warm gloves to wear, and looked for a place for him to spend the night. Of all the places that man could have ended up, he landed in the absolute right place with warm, caring, loving people—and I received a lesson and passed by an opportunity to be Christ to the man. In our lives, what does God wish for us to learn? If we are open and willing to be more like Christ, we are given opportunities. To me this is an example of grace, simply grace. My understandings of grace have been filtered through the lenses of the writings, the sermons, and the life and ministry of John Wesley. Wesley explained grace as prevenient grace, justifying grace, sanctifying grace. These are not three distinct types of grace; instead we experience grace in different ways depending on where we are in relationship with God.

Don't be intimidated by the words; they simply point to the way we experience grace.

Prevenient grace–think convenient or preview.
Justifying grace–think testifying or forgiveness.
Sanctifying grace–think next steps or perfecting.

Prevenient grace is readily available. It is grace that is *convenient* to access and provides us a *preview* of a different life. It's those feelings, nudges, and glimpses of God in our everyday lives. It's the grace that God gives even before we recognize or have awareness of God.

Justifying grace shows we have made a change. We understand that God's forgiveness is available to us now and, in response, we want to live differently. We become aware that God is for us and loves us personally and unconditionally. Our life then *testifies* to a change and to our intentional connection to God and deepening relationship with God. We know and believe that God has and will continue to provide *forgiveness* of our sins.

Sanctifying grace is about moving into a deeper relationship with God and living out that relationship in disciplined practice—"moving on to perfection," as John Wesley would describe it. Not that we are perfect, but we're living in a new way. We treat others with respect, and our lives are characterized by the fruit of the Holy Spirit: love, joy, peace, patience, kindness, generosity, faithfulness, gentleness, and self-control (found in Galatians 5:22-23, NRSV). We take the *next steps* and begin making changes in *perfecting* our relationship with God in service to others.

John Wesley described prevenient grace as the porch of the house, justifying grace as the doorway, and sanctifying grace as the rooms of the house (Wesley 1989).

Prevenient Grace—The Porch

Through prevenient grace, God invites us into the house, but we haven't yet accepted the invitation. We are standing just outside the door.

Justifying Grace—The Door

When we respond to God's invitation, we open the door into God's house. We are made right with God and have assurance that our sins are forgiven, that we are in an intentional relationship with God.

Sanctifying Grace—The Interior

Through justifying grace we enter the house. And once we're there, we find a wealth of rooms to explore. Sanctifying grace is the grace that guides us once we're inside the house, helping us mature in faith and live holy lives. It is through sanctifying grace that we learn more about God and the fullness of life God offers.

In my reflecting about these categories, the image of bread came to me as another way to look at the three descriptions of grace. First, we have to make the bread. Making bread means combining the ingredients—flour, oil, yeast, and water—and mixing them to create the dough, then kneading the dough and adding different ingredients for flavor and texture such as herbs, sesame seeds, or nuts. God's grace is available like the simple, ordinary ingredients of bread. We have different backgrounds. We experience God in different ways, but it is simply grace. In prevenient grace, we are dough, but God is preparing us for something new.

Baking the dough into bread is like justifying grace. The lump of dough becomes something different, something changed, something good. Once we become bread, we are no longer dough. We have reached a new state. We are now bread. We can testify to the change in our life.

Bread on a shelf is simply bread and doesn't do anything for anyone. Bread left on the shelf is useless. We want to be more. Sanctifying grace is like breaking the bread and serving it to others, as we do in Holy Communion. As a broken loaf we find purpose and meaning; in this way, we, with others, lead Christlike lives, as Christ himself was broken for many. As we serve, we become more aware of scripture, seeking the ways of Jesus and praying, in order to communicate with God. We become more loving, more aware of our own needs and the needs of the world. We love God, as Bernard of Clairvaux reminds us, not for our own sake or for the sake of others but for God's sake. We set forth steps to a new path that will bring our lives to complete fullness, thus perfecting our life in God. Then we go forth with others and within others, out into the world, sharing our good news. We live for God and others, and in so doing we are also changed. We move from dough to bread to Holy Communion.

The analogy of dough to bread to Holy Communion makes the point that there are stages along the way. We move along in our faith journey from the nondescript to the sacred. There are different kinds of bread, with different textures and in different sizes and shapes. Likewise, we are different people in different situations with different abilities and talents, but all of us can make ourselves available to help and minister to others. In this way, joined with Christ, we become a living Communion sacrament.

Prevenient Grace–Dough
Justifying Grace–Bread
Sanctifying Grace–Holy Communion

We will look more deeply into each of the forms of grace in the following chapters. Here we are simply talking about grace and how it intervenes in our daily world.

Bishop Kenneth Carder, in a November 2016 *Interpreter* article, wrote,

> The (United Methodist) Book of Discipline defines grace as "the undeserved, unmerited, and loving action of God in human existence through the ever-present Holy Spirit." Grace pervades all of creation and is universally present. Grace is not a gift that God packages and bestows on us and creation. Grace is God's presence to create, heal, forgive, reconcile and transform human hearts, communities and the entire creation. Wherever God is present, there is grace!

We do not have to fully understand how grace works; we just need to continue to be open and willing to accept that God wants to work on and with us. Charles Spurgeon, from a sermon he preached in 1915, helps us understand the mystery.

> Some truths, which it is hard to explain in words, are simple enough in actual experience. No man would refuse to enter a lifeboat because he did not know

> the specific gravity of bodies; neither would a starving man decline to eat till he understands the whole process of nutrition. If you, my reader, will not believe till you can understand all mysteries, you will never be saved at all; accepting pardon through your Lord and Saviour, you will perish in condemnation which will be richly deserved. (Spurgeon 1974)

We begin to understand that grace is like that—we don't need to have everything figured out to appreciate and encounter God in our everyday interactions. We know our lives can be simple and complex at the same time. We do not have to claim all knowledge of God's ways but know that increasing our attentiveness is the first step. We are preparing ourselves for God's grace.

When I was a kid, our church had an auction. The auctioneer was having trouble selling a set of bedsprings, the old style of box springs—not covered with any cloth, just metal coils in a frame. I thought the bedsprings would make a neat trampoline, so I ran to the other side of the church and asked Dad if he could loan me a dollar. He did, and I went back and bought the old bedsprings for a buck. What a deal! In my excitement I ran back to tell Dad of our good fortune. It was then that Dad laughed and explained that he had brought the springs from our basement to get rid of them. Not only had he just paid for what he'd already hauled out of our own basement, but now he was going to have to pay to cart it off to the dump.

God is always moving in our lives,
acting to draw us closer.

God's grace is like that. God not only forgives us for our sins but pays the bill. God hauls the garbage out of our lives, with the price already paid. Our role is to be aware and recognize that grace is freely given and forgiveness is freely available. But even without our awareness, God is always moving in our lives, acting to draw us closer.

In high school I took a chemistry class. During the last class before our Christmas break, the teacher had us work a lab experiment with a partner. We were given the chemical names of items that we needed to combine. We had $C_{12}H_{22}O_{11}$ (table sugar) and NaCl (table salt) and some other items. We combined all these elements, put them in a flat pan, and heated the elements over a Bunsen burner. Happily, the end result was peanut brittle. (Or, in some cases, the results were burnt sugar and salt.) That's simply grace. We combined our willingness to be led through the process with a few common elements. Sometimes it takes a little heat to make a change, to create something new. In hindsight, we can see how God was moving us and combining the right situations with the right people at the right time; and we look back and say, "Sweet. Thanks, God." Grace is like that.

He told them still another parable: "The kingdom of heaven is like yeast that a woman took and mixed into about sixty pounds of flour until it worked all through the dough." Jesus spoke all these things to the crowd in parables; he did not say anything to them without using a parable. So was fulfilled what was spoken through the prophet:

"I will open my mouth in parables,
I will utter things hidden since the creation of the world."
Matthew 13:33-35, NIV

In the next chapters we will unfold God's grace. Like dough forming into bread, we'll look at how the yeast of our lives makes the bread come to life, and likewise, how we feel God working in us. Through parables and life stories we will find the hidden treasures of God's simple yet profound grace.

And we pray,

Lord of opportunities, Lord of examples,
Let us feel your presence each and every day.
Instruct us, show us, make us understand the ways
That you move in our lives.

As we see something as simple as bread
We know that hands have worked to
Combine, mix, knead, and form the bread
To make something good and new.
You have that same desire for us.

Christ of grace, let us know that you're available
In everyday and in many ways,
That you mix up the elements of our simple lives
To make something better than we now know. Amen.

Simply Grace Story: "Middle of My Story" by JS

I grew up Lutheran and belonged to a church in my hometown. It was as good a church as any, I suppose. People came on Sunday morning and left Sunday afternoon. They smiled and drank coffee. They preached of good works and hell-fire. "Repent or die" was one of the reoccurring themes. I didn't go too regularly to church, more of an Easter-and-Christmas type of thing. But even though my dad struggled with his faith, he insisted that I attend Sunday school every week. Church was boring and irrelevant to me. Sunday school was a place where I could at least ask questions, *most of the time.*

I was invited to a youth Super Bowl party. Kind of a big deal for a twelve-year-old nerd with big glasses. I mean, I got to go to a party, with girls. I never had much interest in football, but I was entertained with the happenings of the party. During the halftime show and again after the game, the youth pastor would talk to us about "getting saved" and "accepting Christ." I wasn't sure what he was trying to sell to me.

This middle-aged guy with slick hair and a WWJD bracelet told us about how great life is with Jesus. Life would be better, easier, happier. You'll experience all this joy! The grass certainly sounded greener on that side of the fence. My eyes were big and my ears were open as I listened to him. "You just have to do this one thing. Pray this prayer and *bam*—you're saved." Any preteen kid is going to fall for that sales pitch. "Just repeat after me," said the youth pastor. And just like that, I was in. "Saved."

I was elated for morning to arrive. The sun was going to be

brighter; my parents would have a new car. I'd finally get a dog and a new bike too. This was going to be great! But days passed, and nothing. I kept wondering if I did it wrong. Did I miss a word? Did I pray right? I guess I didn't have a lot of friends . . . Maybe God just didn't like me.

Then, when I was attending a Boy Scout retreat, I got a call. *Heart attack?! What? This can't be right.* My dad had died. He was forty-two. *This isn't happening! A fourteen-year-old boy can't be without his dad.* Granted, we weren't exactly close, but when I grew up we could share more of the same interests. I could show him all the things that would make him proud of me. *What is going on, God?* Certainly, God must have been telling me he doesn't like me. My dad's unexpected death left our family in a dire financial situation. My brothers were out of the house. My mom took on a new job working nights just to make ends meet. I heard talk of having to move. "This is Dad's house; you can't sell it!" I screamed at her. I didn't understand there just wasn't enough money.

There was a lawsuit related to his death being a direct result of a work-related accident. This would allow my mom to collect widow's benefits and we could save the house and our life. But a technicality in the wording of the law took those benefits away. *Are you kidding me?* No house, no car, no bike to ride. God definitely didn't like me, and I didn't like God.

Why do *we* have to struggle for our daily bread? Why is no one helping *us*? I watched my mom leave for work every night at 8 p.m. only to come home exhausted as I left for school at 8 a.m. the next day. When she was diagnosed with Hepatitis C, things really got bad. I was angry, confused. It was God's fault and somehow the church had something to do with it.

My encounters with "Christian people" during those years included ostracism, from having a tattoo. There were no offers of condolences or answers, just the familiar, "God works in mysterious ways," or "God has a plan for us all." For the record, that doesn't offer any comfort to a grieving teen.

My life from this point was mine to live. While I wasn't much with the ladies, online porn was easy and accessible. I didn't have to think about anything when I watched porn. It eased the struggles in my life and made me feel good. Those girls on the screen wanted me, or at least that's what I would tell myself in the dark corner of my room. The need to escape my broken and painful life into a world of fantasy grew daily.

My life spiraled through a series of relationships, a marriage, two kids, and a pile of stress. Porn became my safe haven. I was addicted. Just like a heroin addict does anything to hide their addiction but finds a way to fuel it, that's what I did. I became disconnected.

Being disconnected led to broken wedding vows, an affair, and ultimately a divorce. Even though our marriage had failed years prior to this physical adultery, it was devastating to watch her leave. Everything I knew was gone. My kids. The house we lived in. I was broken inside. Alone. Defeated. How could this have happened? I looked to God for answers. I told God this was a chance to show me he cared about me. Bring her back. Make me feel better. Fix this. *Something*. I can remember the drunken nights driving to nowhere screaming at the dark road ahead. All I heard was silence. God did not exist any longer.

As the party life caught up with me financially, I was forced into a part-time job as a manager at a local fast-food chain. When

I first saw her, I didn't know she was going to change everything. This cute blonde girl with curly hair that had been handcrafted by God (had I believed in God) was far too good for me. The phrase "out of my league" was an understatement.

Our relationship grew. It grew to the point where her aunts and uncles invited us to a family Bible study. I couldn't really say no. That first night was pretty nerve-racking. The host was a strict Baptist family, and heaven help you if you're not a Christian in a Baptist home. Would they see right through me and make me wait in the car? To my surprise, they invited me in—with open arms.

We learned about the fruit of the Spirit: love, peace, perseverance, and faithfulness. I could really understand how people could fall for this stuff. I was longing for it myself. But I knew the truth. Even if God was real, he didn't care about me. I was too far gone to be let into his kingdom. B's aunt asked me one night, "If you were to die tonight, do you think you would go to heaven?" I nearly cried in front of her. I wanted to say yes. "No," I responded. I think her heart was broken too.

The Bible study ended and after a few weeks, I asked B to marry me. She said yes but later confessed something to me that was sobering. I can still feel my heart stop when I think about it. "I'm not sure I can marry someone who isn't a Christian." There it was. She saw through me. I told her that God can't forgive me and I was going to prove it. I spent weeks searching the Bible. Every verse on forgiveness, on salvation, on adultery, and so on. God might love you, but look, God doesn't love me!

As you can imagine I never did find that verse. God didn't ruin my life; I did. He was there the whole time. I was just too busy screaming to hear him. On February 12, 2012, I asked my fiancée to show me how to get saved. We prayed together. Not a "repeat after me" prayer but a real prayer from my heart. I accepted Jesus in my life, for real. I was saved. I *am* saved.

Even though I was saved, I didn't know what it meant to live for Jesus. I didn't understand having a relationship with God. Our finances were out of control. Work became stressful and the daily battles of living with someone else were adding up. We had fights about my baggage, and I was starting to repeat a pattern. Porn was an easy and familiar escape. A place to hide. I kept it secret for a long time. Christian believer in the front, broken-hearted sinner in the back. I was reverting back to who I was. Repeating the pattern over again. God didn't need to concern himself with this; I'll do it on my own. Then when I'm all cleaned up, I'll ask for forgiveness. I didn't understand what God's grace was.

We started attending a different kind of church. Every single Sunday I swear the preacher was talking to me. Teaching me how to get my act together. How to forgive others. How to accept others. How to forgive and accept myself. Every week God pulled me closer to him.

I wanted more information on the church and got connected to one of the campus pastors. I asked him all the hard questions. What about gays in church? What about baptism? What about evolution/creationism? He summed it all up with something that has never left me: "Those aren't salvation issues." That changed the meaning of what church could be for me.

The pastor was excited we were coming to church. I told him I liked the worship but I didn't really like to sing. He smiled and said another thing that's never left me: "Well, maybe if you just make some noise in worshipping the Lord, that'll be cool too." Now you'll see me on Sunday mornings singing loud and proud, even if it's not exactly angelic.

We come to church every week. I've found a small group of men who support me, pray for me, and show me grace. Despite changing careers and paths, we've made the commitment to tithe.

The truth is, I don't know how to end this story. I've come a long way as a believer. I still hold fears of feeling unloved and unaccepted. I guess I'm in the middle of my story and God is always working and revealing himself to me. I rely on God's continual grace guiding me and embracing me. I know that God forgives and continues to forgive. I don't know what the future holds, but I know God has big plans.

Reflection Questions

1. Think about a time that God got your attention. What happened?
2. Wesley describes grace as prevenient, justifying, and sanctifying. What are examples from your own life in these categories, times when you feel that "grace was like that" for you?
3. What does it mean to you that God's grace is freely offered? How do you offer grace freely to others? Why might it be hard to expect nothing in return?
4. Share a time when you gave grace or received grace that was unexpected or without any expectations.
5. Why is it so hard to change our lives even though we know it's what we need to do?

6. Which of these analogies speaks to you more, and why? See pages 16 through 18 for Wesley's porch, doorway, and rooms of a house analogy, or the dough, bread, and Holy Communion analogy.
7. Are you at the beginning, middle, or end of your story with God?

Prevenient Grace

"The grace of God is not complicated or confusing. In fact, it is so simple that many of us miss its true meaning and end up making our lives incredibly complex. I know I did."

—Joyce Meyer, *Closer to God Each Day*

When I was a kid, we used to go exploring along a creek that ran through our town. One spring the snow started to melt and the creek became a small river. It was still cold outside, and we were bundled up in heavy coats, snow pants, and gloves. By one section of the creek there was an old bridge. It extended out into the water a ways, but because the water was high, the bridge did not completely span the entire width to the other side. Being the chubbiest of the crew, my role was to walk out to see if the bridge would hold me, the theory being, if it held the fat kid, it would hold the rest of us. It did hold, for a while, and the next thing I knew I was totally submerged in cold water, and I remember thinking, *This probably isn't a good thing.*

The rushing water held me under, and due to the weight of

the winter garb I struggled to get to the surface. When I did come up, I found that the current had pushed me to the other side of the creek. After I trudged out of the water and onto the shore, I heard the town fire whistle. For those of you who didn't grow up in a small town, the fire whistle signaled supper time. To me this whistle meant simply that I was in big trouble. Grandma had come to visit, and Mom said I had better not be late for dinner.

The only way to get home was to walk to a road bridge about a half mile away and be extremely late for supper. In my fear of being late, I tried to swim back across the creek. I again struggled to the surface because it is hard to swim in a wet coat, snow pants, full boots, and gloves. Oh, by the way, the rest of the group decided not to try the bridge.

Without options, I did walk down to the road bridge, and I did make it home for supper late. When my mom saw a frightened, frozen kid peering at her from icy winter garb, she was not at all mad. She gave me a hug, helped me to warm up, and did not say anything about the time.

God does what God always does—
love.

To me, this is a perfect illustration of prevenient grace. We walk to the edge. We fall. We go under. We fall again. We walk away from God. Something draws us back. We feel that God won't accept us, won't forgive us, won't understand, and might even be angry at us. But God does what God always does—love.

Remember that prevenient grace is the convenient, easily accessible love from God. It's everywhere, it's available, and it pulls us back to God regardless of what we've done. It is grace that comes before all else and is always present, always available. It is also a preview of a better way. That grace is what pulls us, nudges us toward God, and gives us a glimpse of a different life ahead. Wesley talked about "whispers to the heart" that take us from the porch to the doorway to the rooms of the house, or from being simple dough to bread to Holy Communion.

Central to understanding prevenient grace is to understand John Wesley's view of God. Pure and simple, Wesley believed God is love. Wesley's focus is not on our sin nor the fact that we need God because of our sin. The focus begins with love. It comes before all else and embraces us and pulls us to God regardless of our sin, our mistakes, and our missteps. It is also Wesley's belief that grace is active in us and around us. Even before we know God, God loves us. This is not, however, a view that is universally accepted. Some see sin as God's primary emphasis, and this theology focuses on what we do to seek God's forgiveness. Wesley believed the character of God is love. Love comes first and is foremost in our relationship with God. Donald Haynes, in a *United Methodist Reporter* article, encourages us not to see God's love as an abstract philosophy. "God's love is a seeking, whispering, awakening, convicting love" (Haynes, "Taking" 2011).

Wesley's view of a loving God who extends grace is supported throughout the Bible. Jesus describes this seeking, whispering, awakening, and convicting love in three parables in Luke 15—the parables of the lost sheep, lost coin, and lost son.

Luke 15:3-7 Parable of the Lost Sheep

> Then Jesus told them this parable: "Suppose one of you has a hundred sheep and loses one of them. Doesn't he leave the ninety-nine in the open country and go after the lost sheep until he finds it? And when he finds it, he joyfully puts it on his shoulders and goes home. Then he calls his friends and neighbors together and says, 'Rejoice with me; I have found my lost sheep.' I tell you that in the same way there will be more rejoicing in heaven over one sinner who repents than over ninety-nine righteous persons who do not need to repent." (NIV)

I couldn't earn it, and I don't deserve it, still, you give yourself away. Oh, the overwhelming, never-ending, reckless love of God.

"Reckless Love" from Bethel Music

God's love and grace is unearned, undeserved, overwhelming, and never-ending. God's love and grace are seeking. So much so that God will search for the lost and work to bring them home. So much so that God leaves the ninety-nine to search for the one who is lost. That is simply the reckless love of God.

Luke 15:8-10 Parable of the Lost Coin

> "Or suppose a woman has ten silver coins and loses one. Doesn't she light a lamp, sweep the house and search carefully until she finds it? And when she finds it, she calls her friends and neighbors together and

> says, 'Rejoice with me; I have found my lost coin.' In the same way, I tell you, there is rejoicing in the presence of the angels of God over one sinner who repents." (NIV)

We may feel as though we don't matter to God. God is so big and we are insignificant in comparison. We may feel as though God doesn't have time for us or that God won't accept us. God is a seeking God, looking for us in dusty corners until we are found. God pursues us and helps us realize that we each are important, so much so that there will be rejoicing when we're found.

Luke 15:11-32 Parable of the Lost Son

> Jesus continued: "There was a man who had two sons. The younger one said to his father, 'Father, give me my share of the estate.' So he divided his property between them.
>
> "Not long after that, the younger son got together all he had, set off for a distant country and there squandered his wealth in wild living. After he had spent everything, there was a severe famine in that whole country, and he began to be in need. So he went and hired himself out to a citizen of that country, who sent him to his fields to feed pigs. He longed to fill his stomach with the pods that the pigs were eating, but no one gave him anything.
>
> "When he came to his senses, he said, 'How many of my father's hired servants have food to spare, and here I am starving to death! I will set out and go back to my father and say to him: Father, I have sinned against heaven and against you. I am no longer worthy to be called your son; make me like one of your hired servants.' So he got up and went to his father.

> "But while he was still a long way off, his father saw him and was filled with compassion for him; he ran to his son, threw his arms around him and kissed him.
>
> "The son said to him, 'Father, I have sinned against heaven and against you. I am no longer worthy to be called your son.'
>
> "But the father said to his servants, 'Quick! Bring the best robe and put it on him. Put a ring on his finger and sandals on his feet. Bring the fattened calf and kill it. Let's have a feast and celebrate. For this son of mine was dead and is alive again; he was lost and is found.' So they began to celebrate.
>
> "Meanwhile, the older son was in the field. When he came near the house, he heard music and dancing. So he called one of the servants and asked him what was going on. 'Your brother has come,' he replied, 'and your father has killed the fattened calf because he has him back safe and sound.'
>
> "The older brother became angry and refused to go in. So his father went out and pleaded with him. But he answered his father, 'Look! All these years I've been slaving for you and never disobeyed your orders. Yet you never gave me even a young goat so I could celebrate with my friends. But when this son of yours who has squandered your property with prostitutes comes home, you kill the fattened calf for him!'
>
> "'My son,' the father said, 'you are always with me, and everything I have is yours. But we had to celebrate and be glad, because this brother of yours was dead and is alive again; he was lost and is found.'" (NIV)

This parable is the ultimate demonstration of grace, forgiveness, acceptance, and joy. The father offers forgiveness to his son regardless of the son's past decisions, regardless that the son strayed. Donald W. Haynes says it this way: "We can be in and out of a personal relationship with God several times in our life, but God's love never lets us go. We can reject God's love, but God will never reject us" (Haynes, "Wisdom" 2011). It is the awakening and convicting God that makes us realize we want to return to God. Even if our life has gotten away from the loving grace of God, we are always welcome home. God celebrates our return and helps us reset our lives.

I was holding down a button in my car and it said, "Reset values." So I began thinking about times in my life when my reset button was pushed. Certainly, my experiences are not as dramatic as those of the prodigal son or many other people. We all have them, those times when we have to reset our priorities. Marriage and birth of kids are on that list, but I'm also talking about unforeseen events.

When I was fifteen, I was in my one and only (so far) car accident. I hit another car in an intersection and lost my license for 263 days (not that I was counting). It was completely my fault; I wasn't paying attention. It made me more reliant on my parents and friends at the time, of course, but I think the accident made me a better, more aware driver in the long run. That reliance was a reset.

As a junior in high school, I was selected to be a foreign exchange student through a program called American Field Service. I decided to select a country that would be unique or one that I might not ever otherwise visit. So I spent three months living with a family in Ghana, a country in West Africa. This absolutely reset my values.

In one of my first teaching positions, we took turns supervising morning weight lifting. While I was driving to school, I witnessed one of my students and his mom get hit broadside. The other driver missed a four-way stop but did not miss their car. I was the first on the scene. I was trying to talk to the student and then realized his mom was trapped under the dashboard. The student made it; his mom did not. How quickly life can change. Reset can happen in the blink of a missed stop sign.

Three months later, I was in my first principal position. A sixth-grade student was crossing a busy street; an oncoming car did not see the stoplight or the little girl. The priest and I had to get the mom from work and bring her to the hospital. I will never forget that guttural scream when the mom found out her daughter was dead. It also taught me the important role of the church and school in tragic circumstances.

When our mission team was in Haiti during the earthquake, it made me realize how dependent we are on others. It made me realize many things move in and out of our control. As I described it earlier, my time in Haiti was an awakening to prayer, a time I could actually feel the prayers of others. Push reset button now.

About five years ago, I had a major colon resection surgery due to a long history with diverticulitis. Diverticula are pockets in the colon that become infected, and it's cured by massive quantities of antibiotics (or by losing eighteen inches of colon). On a trip to Haiti, a woman came to our clinic who was suffering from diverticulitis. We had antibiotics but not ones that are most effective for this condition. So I gave her the meds I had brought along. At the end of our trip, I developed the same problem and had to beg the only hospital in the area to dig through their pharmacy. My thought at the time: maybe my tombstone could say, "He gave his meds away." Many conditions in our world are fixed by a trip to the corner pharmacy, but across the world these conditions are life-threatening. Push reset.

Honestly, our family has been fairly void of tragic deaths. But it's pretty hard to get through life without the death of people close to us. I have had a best friend die, and when we lose people we frequently interact with and care about deeply, it pushes the reset button.

This past summer I was riding my bike near a local waterfall. I was coming from the top side, so all I could see was calm water before the sheer drop. Calm water before a waterfall. It's just the realization that there will be days ahead that will reset my values. Other times I will simply rely on the knowledge that God's grace is waiting for me, like a warm hug to a frozen, scared child.

You may be asking a couple of questions. Does everyone respond to grace? The simple answer is no. Even though it is available, not everyone turns to or believes in Jesus or God. You might be saying, "I have lived a pretty good life, never cheated on my spouse, never used drugs, tried to be kind to others. Do I need to turn toward grace?" The simple answer is yes. We may like our sins better than other people's sins, but it is simply sin in search of forgiveness in the end.

"Your worst days are never so bad that you are beyond the *reach* of God's grace. And your best days are never so good that you are beyond the *need* of God's grace."

Jerry Bridges, *The Discipline of Grace*

Prevenient grace is that grace that allows us a convenient preview of a new relationship with God. We are like dough, just beginning to take on a new form. It's not that we have it all figured out. It's not that we won't continue to sin and ask for forgiveness.

It's not that all our struggles will end. It is the beginning of sensing a change. Let's walk into it together.

Surely your goodness and unfailing love will pursue me all the days of my life, and I will live in the house of the LORD forever.

Psalm 23:6, NLT

And we pray,

Christ, we come to you as dough.
Knead us, mold us, make us new.
We are grateful for your unrelenting, reckless love.
Help us in this new walk, help us to see you in all things.
There are times we feel lost and doubting.
There are times we feel we've gone under.
Thank you for being on the shore, patiently waiting.
Help us to know you're there. Always there. Amen.

Simply Grace Story: "Nothing Can Separate Us" by Jo

I'm convinced that nothing can separate us from God's love in Christ Jesus our Lord: not death or life, not angels or rulers, not present things or future things, not powers or height or depth, or any other thing that is created.

Romans 8:38-39, CEB

Dick was sexually abused as a little boy, and those horrendous acts against his soul wounded him immensely. Dick was an alcoholic and he was proud of his forty years of sobriety. Dick also suffered bouts of depression and contemplated suicide on more than one occasion.

Each time I heard Dick tell his story to my students, the Holy Spirit worked in and through Dick to transform me. That's the power of community, the power of love, and the power of grace. Like Dick, I too was sexually abused as a little girl, and although I've experienced many dark nights of the soul, through it all, God saved me.

I don't know how young I was when the abuse started—perhaps I was four or five years old, maybe younger. It didn't happen all the time, just some of the time—whenever we went to my grandmother's house for the weekend. My dad was gone for most of my early life. Even when Dad came home from Korea, the abuse continued whenever we'd go for a weekend visit to Grandmother's house. My abuser was my uncle, my dad's oldest brother. Uncle E never married and lived with my grandparents. Everybody said he was an alcoholic.

The sexual abuse is still too distasteful for me to talk about it publicly. Just know that my uncle sexually, mentally, and emotionally abused me. You may be wondering—*Where was Jesus when all of this was going on?* I will tell you that Jesus was right there with me—and every time my uncle slayed me, he slayed Jesus too. Unexpectedly, Uncle E died shortly after I turned nine. Prior to his death, I never told anyone about the abuse, other than my best friend, Lisa, who was only one year older than me. Neither one of us knew exactly what to do. So, we just kept the secret between ourselves—best friends forever—even to this very day.

I was ten, almost a year after Uncle E's death, when my mother ordered a series of booklets purposed to help me understand the facts of life, you know, the "birds and the bees." So, I read the booklets and, for the first time, I grasped what Uncle E did to me. Naively, I assumed I was pregnant. Again, I told Lisa, my best friend. Still, we didn't know what to do! So I went to bed that night petrified and scared to death. I cried with my head buried in my pillow so as not to make any noise.

On one evening, my mom came into my bedroom, as she always did, to offer a good night's kiss and discovered me crying. Mom asked, "What's the matter? Why are you crying?" I blurted out, "I'm pregnant!" Then I sat on the foot of my bed and told my mom, in detail, how Uncle E, who had been dead for almost a year, had sexually abused me. My sister was there because we shared the same room. She heard everything. Mom turned to her and asked if Uncle E had done anything to her and she said, "No. Nothing."

I think that was the longest night of my life. When the interview stopped, the drama began. Then, everybody knew what had happened to me—my mother, father, brothers, sister, grandparents, aunts, uncles, cousins, and neighbors. *Everyone* knew what Uncle E did to me. Everyone was angry, but there was no one to punish because he was already dead. There was a lot of chaos, uproar, disbelief, and shame going around. Mom and Dad openly argued and debated the matter. Ultimately, Dad said that he couldn't believe that his brother would do such a thing.

My father's words were clear. They cut me deeply, creating a gaping wound that bled for many years. In my parents' ignorance, there was no doctor's visit, no police report, no investigation, no counseling. No nothing! There was just a little girl—me—who felt abandoned, ashamed, humiliated, isolated, and disgraced. There was nothing, absolutely nothing, except for God's grace! In the book of Isaiah, the prophet tells us, "Cry for help and you'll find its grace and more grace. The moment he hears, he'll answer" (Isaiah 30:19, my paraphrase).

Did you know only 11 percent of child sexual abuse (CSA) incidents are committed by a stranger? The majority of CSA incidents happen in relationship with a family member or someone else known by the child or family. In years gone by, law enforcement taught "stranger danger," but we had it wrong because the majority of the time the sex offender is *not* a stranger but someone who lives right under our noses!

Years later, I remember sitting on a grassy hillside and staring across the landscape of the college campus for what seemed like hours. I was perplexed and distraught. There was an anger inside of me that was raging like a storm. I looked up and yelled at God, "What in the world am I supposed to do?" Immediately, a black and white police car drove past, and a female was driving the car. She rolled up to the stop sign; the window was down. She had blonde hair and it was up in a French braid. She came to a stop, with her blinker on, and she made a right turn and drove out of sight. It was no more than a five-second encounter. I thought, *That's what I'll do. I'll be a police officer.* That week I applied, and a few months later, after training, they hired me.

I should have gotten on my knees, but instead, I "copped" an attitude. I had a chip on my shoulder. I thumbed my nose up at God and church. Pride and anger got in my way; I focused on my circumstances and not on God. I decided that I knew what was best for my life. I was hurt and mad and became defiant; the storm within me erupted. I went into police work and never looked back. I fell a long way from God's grace, as if I had jumped off the Empire State Building.

For about ten years of my life, throughout my twenties, I lost my way. I stopped walking in the presence of Jesus. I saw and experienced things that caused my heart to grow cold and calloused. I became indifferent to God. Police work exposed me to a dark side of humanity. My faith weakened slowly. I didn't pray. I didn't read my Bible. I didn't go to church.

When I look back on my life, I realize that police work was a good fit for me. I had the ability to set my emotions aside and not let anything touch me. The numbness came naturally for me. I was a good cop. I did my job well, but in those early days of my career, I was lost. I was alone. I was afraid, and no one but God knew how dark my soul felt.

During this dark time of my life, I got pregnant out of wedlock and had an abortion. I was in and out of several relationships, and police work was the only thing that made sense in my life. My personal life was a wreck; but I thought, *I have my job, I can make it. I can survive.*

I remember sitting in my squad car on a gravel road. It was early morning about 3:00 a.m., and I started thinking about everything. It all came back and piled up like a ton of bricks on my shoulders—the sexual abuse, my father not believing me, my mother not protecting me, my family emotionally abandoning me, the church turning me away, failed relationships, abortion, divorce . . . I concluded that I was a failure. I pulled my .357 Smith & Wesson Magnum out of my holster, stuck it in my mouth, and tried to pull the trigger, but God wouldn't let me. I yelled at God and told him to just leave me the hell alone.

Then, I got a radio call from headquarters. I holstered my gun and picked up the mic. They dispatched me to a domestic disturbance at a trailer park. I acknowledged the call, wiped my face, and responded to the call. When I got there, this couple—a guy and a girl—were arguing because the guy caught her "running around" on him. He was crying and carrying on. I ended up cuffing him and putting him in the back seat of my squad car.

On the way to the jail, I kept looking in my rearview mirror at his face. I could feel his pain. I started crying with him because I knew exactly how he felt. I pulled over and stopped my car, opened the back door, and told him to get out of my car. Then I told him to turn around and I took the cuffs off him. I stood on the side of the road crying with and hugging this man whom I had arrested. I told him that I was sorry that his girlfriend cheated on him. I let him go and asked him not to go back to the house that night. He promised me that he wouldn't go back there, and then I drove away and back to the gravel road.

Again, I pulled my gun out and put it in my mouth. I knew that letting the man go was totally improper, but I didn't care. I didn't care about anything. But again, God wouldn't let me pull the trigger.

In my brokenness, I realized Jesus loves me despite all my sins and all my failings—despite everything that I did and failed to do. Jesus loves me—unconditionally—no matter what. God doesn't love us because we're good, or even because we're worthy. God is in us because Christ is in us, and nothing can separate us from the love of Christ. That night I began a new journey.

I moved to Florida in 1989, and in 1990, Tony and I met. Three years later, we married in December 1993. For the first time in my life, with God's help, I was able to give my heart completely to another person—unconditionally. I trusted him. He helped me work through some of the issues I had from being sexually abused as a child. We made it a priority to pray and to go to church. In 2005, God led us to South Dakota, where I eventually became chief of police for eight years.

Have you ever noticed what Jesus does when you give him a loaf of bread? He reaches out—he takes the bread—he blesses it—he breaks the bread and gives it. And so it is with my life and yours. Jesus takes us—he blesses us—he breaks us—and he shares us—he uses us—works in, with, and through us to fulfill God's purpose for our lives.

God led me to begin preaching after my retirement from law enforcement. God led us to create a fund to benefit children who disclose sexual abuse to law enforcement. The child/caregiver can begin the healing process at a horse ranch through a program called Hope, Healing, and Hoof Prints. We began an organization named Hope in God, a Christian network of women survivors of child sexual abuse and sexual assault, who provide spiritual and emotional support. Hope in God also serves as a resource for law enforcement, churches, increasing community awareness, and providing support to survivors of child sexual abuse. These initiatives have evolved into Divine Providence of South Dakota. The mission is "To lead people, especially those wounded by child sexual abuse and sexual assault into a thriving relationship with Jesus Christ and to strengthen churches in Northeast South Dakota."

In the center of the tempests of life, we can find a place of quiet communion in the Holy Spirit. That is the place where God dwells and where there is perfect peace. But how do we get there? How do we stay hopeful after being wounded? How do we pass through the turmoil—the hurt—the anger—the shame—the brokenness—the humiliation of child sexual abuse? Jesus sought and saved me on a gravel road.

We keep our eyes fixed on Jesus—to begin to know him and to allow God to reveal himself to us. I want you to know that God loves you and that his mercy and grace are greater than any of your circumstances or your sins. We need not fear because everywhere our Savior leads us, the grace of God precedes us. Have the full assurance that nothing can separate us from the love of God in Jesus Christ.

Reflection Questions

1. Think of a time when you felt you were in deep waters. What and who helped you through that time?
2. God delights in finding the lost. How could you step out and help others who may be lost?
3. Keep a list of resets in your life. What were they and how did they change your perspective?
4. Like many parables, Jesus doesn't provide the ending. Reread the parable of the lost son. Do you think the older son joined the party? Write the ending to this parable.
5. Have you ever felt beyond the love or forgiveness of Christ? Does prevenient grace begin to help you understand better?

Justifying Grace

"I do not at all understand the mystery of grace—only that it meets us where we are but dœs not leave us where it found us."

—Anne Lamott, *Small Victories*

Parable of the Bridges

In the Land of Old, in a place far, far away was a beautiful country—rolling hills of trees and orchards producing more than the people could use or eat; rolling hills of farmland producing more food than the country could eat.

In the Land of Old lived the People of the Trees and the People of the Land. The People of the Trees were tall and strong and spent their time growing wood to build homes and fruit to eat. The People of the Land were short and strong and spent their time tending to their fields growing vegetables every color of the rainbow. While they were not enemies, they had little to do with each other.

Two bridges crossed a raging, angry river. The People of the Trees made a bridge of wood from their forest. The People of the Land made a bridge made from the soil of their fields. There was no way to get to the trees and there was no way to get to the fields without crossing a bridge over the raging, angry river.

One day a great rain came to the land. It rained for days and nights. It rained so much it looked like you were standing under a great waterfall. It rained so hard that the bridge of the People of the Land was no more. The soil was swallowed by the dark, cross river.

When the rains stopped, the People of the Land came to the wooden bridge built by the People of the Trees, ready to cross to their fields. "No, no, no," said the King of the People of the Trees. "You must pay to cross on our bridge."

"Why should we pay?" said the People of the Land.

"You don't have to pay if you want to cross on your dirt bridge, but if you want to cross our wooden bridge, it will be one gold coin each," grinned the King.

The People of the Land screamed and shouted, but in the end, there was no way to get to their fields, so after much grumbling and gnashing of teeth, they paid their gold coins.

Soon the People of the Trees grew very wealthy, as well as fat and lazy. So lazy, in fact, that they decided to hire the Tiny Folk to collect the gold coins at the wooden bridge. The first morning the Tiny Folk stood at the bridge, the People of the Land laughed. "How will you stop us?" they asked.

The Tiny Folk replied, "We will not stop you, but it will be a bad decision to not pay the gold coin."

"Out of the way," shouted one man as he pushed through the crowd. "I won't pay these Tiny Folk." As the man was halfway across the wooden bridge, the Tiny Folk on the other side shook the bridge and this man of the land fell into the irritated river, never to be seen again.

"And because of this man's folly, the rest of you will have to pay one gold coin *and* one rock each to pass across the wooden bridge. Pay us the coin and throw your rock into the cave on the other side." Despite the added burden and knowing they had no choice, with great sadness, the People of the Land paid a golden coin and each threw one rock into the cave every time they crossed.

This went on for many years. The People of the Trees grew fatter and lazier. Their trees became lazy too and stopped producing enough fruit for lack of fertilizer and pruning. But the People of the Trees didn't care because they had so much money and could buy their food elsewhere. The People of the Land grew angrier because they had to grow more and more vegetables to have enough money to pay their toll. They were angry because the fat and lazy People of the Trees were ruining their lives.

One morning, a great group of Tiny Folk met the People of the Land at the bridge. "Today," said their leader, "may be your last toll." The people were so consumed with anger and sorrow that some did not hear the tiny leader. Again, the leader said, "Today may be your last toll. For many years you were asked to give a coin and a rock. The money has gone to people who have become fat and lazy. Look at their trees. They are broken and full of bugs. The trees don't produce fruit like they did in the old days. Now look at your fields. Each day you took rocks from your fields and now your vegetables are as big as small children. And there is a pile of rocks in that cave for you to build a bridge." Build a bridge they did, made out of the rocks of their fields. It was stronger than a bridge of dirt.

Meanwhile, the People of the Trees had grown so lazy that they let their bridge go to pot. Their bridge was in disrepair, with splinters and cracks, ready to crash into the mean, rushing river. And their trees had grown so weak that there was no useable wood to build another bridge.

But the People of the Land could not forgive and made the People of the Trees pay one gold coin to cross the stone bridge. The Land People grew fat and lazy. So lazy that they hired the Tiny Folk to take the coins. Shortly afterward the leader of the Tiny Folk demanded one gold coin and one nut from a tree to pass across the bridge. And when the Tiny Folk gave the nuts back to the People of the Trees, they planted the nuts, which became trees, which became a new wooden bridge. So when the rock bridge eventually gave in to the rains and the raging, angry river . . . and so it goes. And so it goes. And so it goes.

At some point in our lives, we must decide we want something different. We have to decide that the old ways won't do any longer. We have to decide to take up God's offer to live a different, better way. We reach a bridge, a doorway, a fork in the road. It occurs to us that our anger and resentment are only hurting us. They blind us to new opportunities and new possibilities of living together in God's blessed community. We want to be forgiven and offer forgiveness to others. We want freedom from the anger that consumes us. And when we make that decision, we accept God's grace and take a different form. When we die to the old and are born to the new, we are new people, and we can testify that God is doing something new in us as individuals and as people of faith. We are justified through grace and restored to a right relationship with God. We are made right with God. We are saved.

I need to come clean. God has granted me the gift of doubt,

closely followed by the gifts of suspicion and disbelief. These "gifts" served me well as a science teacher, a school principal, and a parent, but sometimes not so well as a Christian. I've always wanted to know how things work and the details behind the details. My doubt drives my curiosity, so it's a keen tool. But doubt sometimes puts me on a cycle similar to the People of the Land and the People of the Trees, where my faith is tested.

So if anyone is in Christ, there is a new creation: everything old has passed away; see, everything has become new!

2 Corinthians 5:17, NRSV

I have been envious and at the same time mistrustful of people who have no uncertainty about the existence of God. Because I have the spiritual gift of doubt. While I see grace in my life and that of others, could it just be a series of happy circumstances? Yet I have hope, not because I can see or because I understand completely, but because I choose to have faith. I also understand why you might doubt. Maybe these aren't adequate analogies, but many things we do in life require risk and leaps of faith. Why do you become a parent, even though you have no idea what it is like to have and raise a child? Why do you get on a bike or a skateboard or learn to drive a car? Why do you ask someone on a date or later to marry you? Why do you go on that first mission trip or first volunteer to help others?

When you marry someone, you commit to a future together, even though you can't see what is ahead. And I can say after being married for so many years, that my spouse continues to surprise me. I thought I knew what I was getting into when we married, but I had no idea. You can't understand what it's like to be intimately related to a person until you take that leap of faith into the commitments that come with marriage. Likewise, I loved our children even as they grew in my wife's womb, but I'm still learning how to be a more loving parent.

The most important things in life can't be seen, measured, predicted, or completely explained. There are also holy things that have happened in my life that I can't explain. I have felt the presence of God for which I have no alternate explanation. There are people who have said the right thing or done the right thing who feel divinely ordained. So I've taken the leap of faith and trusted God despite my doubt and sometimes because of my doubt.

While I don't go nearly enough, I am a scuba diver. My most recent dive was in Roatan, Honduras. We saw a shipwreck, turtle, grouper, and all kinds of other amazing fish and coral. At one point, when I was about eighty feet underwater I looked up. Wow. There was a whole lot of water between the surface and me. If I panicked and swam to the surface, I would face a host of issues, due to decompression that could make me very sick, or worse. So I simply said to myself, "Trust. Everything you need to live is right here." This is my mantra for my faith journey. Trust. Everything you need to live is right here, with a loving, grace-filled, forgiving God. When you cross over the doorstep into justifying grace, you have to leap; you have to trust.

We began with the convenient grace from God. We saw a preview of a different life ahead. When we reach the doorstep, we testify to a change in our life and ask God for forgiveness for our sins. We're now baked bread and we've changed our form. Prevenient grace has prepared us for justifying grace.

When we are justified by God's grace, we are changed because a right relationship with God cannot help but make us different. We respond by showing our change. We understand that God's forgiveness is available, and we want to live differently. We *testify* to this change, and we trust that God has been and will continue to provide *forgiveness* of our sins.

First United Methodist Church, Wichita Falls, Texas, includes a section of Distinctive Wesleyan Doctrines on their website (www.fumcwf.org/wesleyan-doctrines) that explains justifying grace this way:

> Justifying grace causes a relational change between ourselves and God. We are brought to realize and trust (have faith) that we are restored to relationship with God. We come to know that we are God's children, and we are forgiven. As justifying text in a word processor or on a typewriter aligns the text in a certain way (i.e. right or left justified), justifying grace aligns us with God. In that alignment, we become new creatures in Christ. We believe that sometimes justification comes about instantaneously; sometimes it is a gradual process. Either way, it is a new beginning; it is not an end.

Randy Maddox, in his book *Responsible Grace*, indicates that "Wesley defined justification in one word: forgiveness." It begins with "a simple recognition of our sinfulness and helplessness" and that this conviction is simply a gift from God and a response to prevenient grace. We begin with a "sincere desire to cease doing evil," sensing the need to make "an entire change of heart and life."

The official website for the United Methodist Church (www

.umc.org) includes a section that is noted by *Our Wesleyan Heritage* and offers this:

> This process of salvation involves a change in us that we call conversion. Conversion is a turning around, leaving one orientation for another. It may be sudden and dramatic, or gradual and cumulative. But in any case, it's a new beginning. Following Jesus' words to Nicodemus, "You must be born anew" (John 3:7, RSV), we speak of this conversion as rebirth, new life in Christ, or regeneration.
>
> . . . John Wesley called this process justification. Justification is what happens when Christians abandon all those vain attempts to justify themselves before God, to be seen as "just" in God's eyes through religious and moral practices. It's a time when God's "justifying grace" is experienced and accepted, a time of pardon and forgiveness, of new peace and joy and love. Indeed, we're justified by God's grace through faith.
>
> Justification is also a time of repentance—turning away from behaviors rooted in sin and toward actions that express God's love. Because of this we can expect to receive assurance of our present salvation through the Holy Spirit "bearing witness with our spirit that we are children of God" (Romans 8:16).

The process of justifying grace involves a conversion experience. Some refer to it as rebirth, new life, being born again, or regeneration. One of the interesting facets of John Wesley is that of his own conversion. Wesley reluctantly attended a group Bible study meeting on Aldersgate Street in London. The leader of the meeting was describing "the change which God works in the heart," and Wesley described that he felt his own heart "strangely warmed." It was not a dramatic conversion event. But note this: Wesley believed in

God before Aldersgate. He was a baptized Christian, but he experienced God in a new way at Aldersgate. It was a reset moment for Wesley. At Aldersgate, Wesley realized that God loved him, and this empowered Wesley's mission for the rest of his life, but all his previous experiences before led him to that moment of realization. That was my experience.

When I was in middle school, I attended a church camp. There was a campfire one night and people were asked to give their life to Christ. I remember people crying, running around, praying, and apparently accepting Christ into their life. I found the whole experience confusing, a bit scary, and I really was not sure what was happening.

As a preacher's kid (PK), anything short of my personal death was not a valid excuse to miss church. I made a pledge that once I got to college, I would not grace the doorstep of a church. I was actually quite successful in that promise. Toward the end of my college years, I began to miss the community of a church. There was a pull to return.

A faith journey never has a straight trajectory; rather, it's a long, winding path with twists and turns, hills and valleys.

After college I started my first job, was married, and began to attend church regularly. My wife and I became more active in the church, including teaching Sunday school and serving in various capacities. Unlike some people, I can't point to a date for a spiritual conversion experience. It was more like Wesley's experience;

my heart was strangely warmed. Over the years, my connection to my faith has grown, but it was not a straight trajectory; rather, it's been a long, winding path with hills and valleys. I have also increasingly realized and become more grateful that God has not given up on me. Justification is all about testifying to a change and about forgiveness.

My dad served churches in a number of communities, but early in his ministry, he served a church in a German/Russian community that had developed their own list of the Seven Deadly Sins. My father related the following story:

> Their list of sins included the usual ones of drinking, smoking, and chewing, but they added a couple of their own. To play with a regular deck of cards was a sin because they were the "devil's cards." Dancing was also added to the sin list.
>
> This community celebrated high school graduation with a big senior banquet, held on a Saturday. It was the highlight of the year for the students, school, and families. The place was decorated elaborately. Families brought their best tableware and the mothers prepared a delicious meal with all the trimmings. The students were served as if they were at the famous Waldorf-Astoria hotel. The graduates were all dressed in formals and tuxes, and I was chosen to be the entertainment, giving a nice speech with lots of jokes. The banquet closed with the Grand March. The couples made circles around the gym while being introduced. My wife and I were given the honor of leading the Grand March.
>
> Remember the senior banquet was on Saturday. When I came to the church on Sunday morning one of the parishioners met me at the door. He told me

> that I was a minister of the devil, because we led the Grand March, which is dancing—and dancing was a sin. He and his wife and their family were leaving the church right there and right now.
>
> I was so filled with guilt that this family left the church. On the next Sunday morning, I drove to their farm at six o'clock in the morning and told them I did not believe I had sinned, that I was not a minister of the devil, and asked for his forgiveness for hurting and disappointing him so deeply.
>
> He refused to shake my hand and said, "I will not forgive you, and you can leave my farm right now."
>
> We moved to another parish. Two years later, the man who left the church sought me out, driving over two hundred miles to meet me. With great emotion, he apologized for not accepting the offer of forgiveness.
>
> Now you need to remember a few things, how rigid and dogmatic Germans from Russia could be. Men didn't hug each other—men only shook hands.
>
> With tears flowing down each other's faces, this man and I hugged each other, right there in broad daylight with a bunch of people around, offering and receiving each other's forgiveness. I have never done anything similar since. I am the poorer person for not doing so.

We all make decisions and have deep-seated feelings. We say and do things we regret. We make mistakes. God keeps working on us, nudging us to a better place. We seek and respond to God's prodding. We take the step, the leap of faith. We respond to justifying grace, and we move toward God's warm embrace.

And we pray,

God of new beginnings
Help me to step off my treadmill

And walk toward you,
Toward forgiveness and your warm embrace.

Help me know you are alongside my path
Even when I walk astray, you're there.
Thank you for my awakening, my awareness
As I testify to your goodness in my life. Amen.

Simply Grace Story: "My Grace" by Grant

For as long as I can remember, I have been a believer. I have attended church regularly, gone to catechism, given offerings, attended Sunday school, and participated in youth group. What I didn't fully understand is that whenever and whatever, God's grace is there.

Even though I prayed every day, I was not a true follower until what happened a few years ago. Sure, I believed in God and that anything was possible, but I didn't truly understand, until it was literally and physically thrown in my face.

In May 2011, I married my soul mate. Then around July 2011 we were excited to announce that we were pregnant! A couple months later my wife called to me, as she thought her water had broken. *What?* To my deep concern, her water had broken and unfortunately too soon in the pregnancy.

As we sat there waiting for the doctor, I was convinced that nothing was wrong. The doctor came in and stated that there was little to no fluid around the baby. After a few days of bed rest, my wife was admitted into the high-risk OB unit. I remember sitting there wondering, *Why?*

The next three weeks we sat in the hospital, listening to the constant *whoosh whoosh* of our baby's heartbeat. One night, as I sat on my wife's bedside, we decided that this unborn baby's middle name would include "Grace." Because of God's grace, she was still here, and we looked forward to meeting her!

At twenty-six weeks, to the day, it was time. My wife was wheeled off to surgery and I was wearing an awesome gown so that I could be part of the whole procedure. Going into the surgical area, there was a curtain between upper and lower torso. There were easily fifteen people waiting on the other side of the room.

The surgeon did his work and soon I saw this "thing" being carried to the other side of the room. As a "micro-preemie," it truly looked more like a thing than a baby. The medical team switched into high gear, and after a few minutes told us our thing was a baby girl. We would spend a lot of time with our baby in the Neonatal Intensive Care Unit (NICU).

On the way home that night, I prayed, "God, please, whatever you can do, please have my daughter live!" On another night driving home, I was very angry. I pounded my steering wheel and yelled out, "God, if you are truly there, let my baby be OK! What have I done wrong?" A few days later, the song "Who Am I?" came on the radio:

> Not because of what I've done,
> But because of who you are.

I stopped. I asked God for his grace and mercy for my child and wife. I asked for God's grace, understanding, and healing for my child.

One hundred and twenty-six days later, we celebrated going home with our little girl. Maci Lynn Grace. I will never forget that day! After five months in the Neonatal Intensive Care Unit, life was beginning to get back to normal.

A few months later my wife was doing well, but she was losing weight, and we knew something just wasn't right. After some discussion and convincing, she went in for a general physical. Her bloodwork was off, and she was referred to an oncologist. I remember driving home and pounding on my steering wheel. Again, I asked God, "Why?" and then pulled over and prayed. I prayed for healing and for grace for what we were about to go through.

Another battle was in front of us—stage IV Hodgkin's lymphoma. My steering wheel took a pounding again. "Why God?" But I prayed for healing and for grace, for what we were about to go through. After twelve treatments and a weeklong hospital stay, we learned a lot about this disease. After a bone marrow biopsy, it was decided that the cancer was not gone and we were referred to a doctor in Omaha who specializes in this cancer.

We hoped and prayed for a miracle. I asked God to guide us and secretly asked for a miracle and grace upon us. As we listened to this specialist, he stated that he could not find any cancer. To be sure, we decided to perform yet another bone marrow biopsy to determine that there was no cancer. A week later, no cancer was to be found!

We often say that something happens by God's grace and mercy. We often use the word *grace* in so many sentences and Facebook messages. What does that exactly mean? I asked for God's grace. Free and unmerited favor of God, resulting in the salvation of sinners and the bestowal of blessings. So simply stated, but very hard to do.

I found that as a sinner, I am saved by God's love toward sinners and that God bestows blessings. It doesn't always work this way, but I am a person who has asked for God's grace and received it. God does not always provide proof of grace. But I see my proof of grace every day, in a growing girl and a beautiful wife. All we can do is pray, believe, and find the grace that is provided in our lives. And make sure to buy vehicles with sturdy steering wheels.

Reflection Questions

1. Are you on or have you been on a loop like the People of the Land and People of the Trees? How can you break the chain of resentment, mistakes?
2. Think about your conversion experience. Can you mark a date or time, or was it more of a gradual awareness?
3. Is there someone you need to forgive? How can you take steps to make that happen?
4. Think about bread—the various types, styles, smells, taste, texture, the process of baking. How might this be an example of different ways people come to Christ?
5. Share a time when God answered your prayer.
6. Think back on the Simply Grace Story above. Why might God not always provide proof of grace?
7. Start a prayer list. Include people you can pray for every day and why you are praying for them.

Sanctifying Grace

Therefore, if anyone is in Christ, the new creation has come: The old has gone, the new is here!
2 Corinthians 5:17, NIV

Over the past couple of years, I've enjoyed riding my bike more regularly. There is a nice bike trail near where we live, a beautiful nineteen-mile loop around the city. I like several things about the trail. It follows a river and has some inviting scenery. It is fairly level. Often I see birds and wildlife on the trail; I've raced geese, chased deer, and watched a kingfisher dive for lunch.

But, for the most part, I like the route that I take. It's always easy at the beginning; your legs feel fresh and there's a lot to see. When you get to the most remote, windiest part of the trail, it's about the same distance to turn around or finish, so you might as well just plod ahead. The one stretch that's uphill and the final stretch are both in high-traffic areas, motivating me to not look like a fat old man biking, even though I'm a fat old man biking.

There is one segment of the trail that is always interesting to me. It's downhill and a pretty good drop. You can pick up a lot of speed and rest a bit. After a steep decline, it levels off for maybe a hundred yards, and then there's a slight incline before the next section where you're going downhill again. That small uphill always seems way too hard. You're cruising down and then this almost unexpected and more difficult stretch comes into play.

Where are you on the path of sanctifying grace?

We've begun the path of sanctifying grace. It's usually an easy start. We make the decision to live differently and we begin the phase of a new life. It feels easy until there are some hills. Wind blows in our face and our pace slows. There are some unexpected bumps along our path that maybe seem worse because things *had* been going smoothly. But we don't turn back; we continue forward. We continue surrounded by a great cloud of witnesses and with hope. We've begun a new, sometimes unexpected, serendipitous path into sanctifying grace.

We have gone from the porch through the doorway and are now exploring the rooms of God's love. We have gone from dough to bread, and now we are exploring Holy Communion. We are now part of an important sacrament; we're living in and through the lives of others and living out a life in the model of Jesus Christ.

Holy Communion in the United Methodist Church is considered an "open table" that allows anyone to receive the cup, symbolic of the blood of Christ, and bread, symbolic of the body of Christ. In our liturgy we say that Christ invites us to his table. The invitation is not for a particular denomination, and participants don't have to be a particular age. Church membership is not required. The invitation is for "all who love him [Christ], who earnestly repent of their sin, and seek to live in peace with one another."

For those of us who are living into sanctifying grace, Holy Communion is a reminder and celebration of Jesus and his sacrifice for us. It's a time to realign our priorities and be grateful. One of my favorite Holy Communion memories was during a trip to Haiti. It was World Communion Sunday, a Sunday designated for people around the globe to share in Communion together and remember Christ's gift to us all. I knelt at the altar with a Haitian man on one side and a Haitian woman on the other side. The scene is still so vivid for me, and I thought, *Now this is what World Communion Sunday is all about*. We were living out God's love and grace by sharing the bread and the cup with others across the world.

A few years ago, I visited a donor's house. This woman had been a small but consistent donor to the organization that I worked for at the time. The woman had described how she decided to turn the heat down this winter so she could donate more to missions. Then, as we sat around her kitchen table, she brought out the best she had—store-bought cookies and coffee. It was surprisingly holy for me. I felt the body of Christ in lemon cookies and the blood of Christ in weak Folger's coffee. This woman testified to me through her faithfulness and commitment, with a humble, yet powerful, witness. If we're open to God, we can take Communion in many forms. It can be part of a formal worship service, and it can happen in our everyday lives. We live out our faith and continue to learn from the faith of others.

Sanctifying grace is about moving into a new relationship with God and living out that relationship in Christian practices, which include Bible study, prayer, fasting, caring for the poor and disposed, visiting the sick and those in prison, acts of justice and compassion, worship, and of course, Holy Communion. We take the next steps and begin making changes in order to perfect our relationship with God as God completes God's work in us. Through sanctifying grace, we have entered a lifelong journey of living the example of Christ.

"We hold that the wonder of God's acceptance and pardon do not end God's saving work, which continues to nurture our growth in grace."

The United Methodist Book of Discipline

Randy Maddox, in his book *Responsible Grace: John Wesley's Practical Theology*, considers the steps to sanctifying grace and the "gradual nature of salvation and the interrelationships of different facets." Furthermore, "[Wesley] saw Christian life as a continuing journey into increasing depths of 'grace upon grace.' . . . For him the following aspects of human salvation were not an ordered series of discrete states; they are intertwined facets of an overarching purpose—our gradual recovery of the holiness that God has always intended for us." Or as the Wichita First United Methodist Church website puts it:

> We hold that the wonder of God's acceptance and pardon (justification) is not the end or ultimate goal of God's saving work. Rather, it is just the beginning of living out the life of faith. Through the action of the Holy Spirit, God continues to nurture our growth in

> grace in a continual journey toward "having the mind of Christ and walking as he walked." John Wesley would say this is our "going on to perfection."
>
> We start the work to understand the impact of our path from prevenient grace to justifying grace to sanctifying grace.

I think one of the most important aspects of these definitions of grace is, it's a journey. We are thankful for the grace that God provides, so we can show grace to others. We reflect on the influences on our path, and we take intentional steps to move toward a more Christlike life. We may never reach it, but we are moving toward a more perfect example; we are living our life in faith. While it's not a straight-line path, we more fully understand grace.

While thinking and writing about these stages of grace, my wife and I took a trip to Mexico. One day we were walking in an area with many shops and merchants, and I came upon a twenty-peso bill lying on the cobblestone. I looked around and no one was near. A couple came walking toward me and one of them said, "Hey, it's all yours, man."

I picked up the note and handed it to a street vendor and told him to have a good day. It occurred to me that this exchange was like grace—an unexpected, undeserved, unmerited gift. After strolling through the market area, we lounged by the ocean.

Then it hit me like a coconut falling from a tree, this wasn't *anything* like God's grace. God doesn't choose those who do and don't receive grace; it's available to *everyone*. God doesn't choose the woman selling bracelets and ignore the man selling sea shells. Everyone has the opportunity to receive grace, regardless of country of origin, race, gender, or lot in life—grace is even available to beach chair loungers. Then later, when I found out the twenty-peso note is only worth about one US dollar, I definitely knew the encounter wasn't anything like grace. God doesn't dole out grace in small bills; rather, God is open-handed and generous, and God's gift is never-ending.

To reach the stage of sanctifying grace, there are influences and factors that guide us along this trail. Some main influences in my life include my grandfather, a simple farmer who did prison ministry until late in his life and always opened family gatherings with scripture-reading and prayer; my parents, who are avid readers, and mentors and supporters, and who provide me with thoughtful feedback; and my wife, who is the disciplined Bible scholar of the family, willing to put up with my continual thoughts and ideas du jour.

This may sound strange, but one of the biggest influences for solidifying my life as a Christian was a Jewish family. My dad was appointed to another church in June, but I stayed in the town where we had been living so I could work for the summer before heading off to college that fall. I stayed and lived with my best friend and his family—a Jewish family. Throughout our friendship my friend invited me to be a part of Jewish holidays and celebrations. This family has largely been responsible for keeping a small synagogue open in northern South Dakota. Through our friendship I learned a lot about the history and symbolism of their faith. I learned what tradition means to a religion. Mostly I learned the importance of Jesus to my own faith journey. I couldn't dismiss Jesus as just another prophet, and this insight solidified my connection to Jesus Christ and to Christianity.

Lee Strobel, in his book *The Case for Grace*, conducted a series of engaging interviews with various people. In one chapter titled

"The Professor," Strobel reconstructs a dialogue with Craig Hazen, who has studied world religions, and said, "The Christian view of grace sets it apart from all other religions, there's no doubt about it." Later in the chapter, Hazen states, "Christianity is unique. Its teachings on grace are unparalleled in world religions." There are religious traditions that promote going through stages or steps in an effort to reach God. Christianity is unique in that grace is offered to both the lifelong Christian and the person who gives their life to Christ on their deathbed. Grace is about what God does, not what we do to try to reach God.

This is a statement that I know will not be readily accepted by some Christians, but I'm not sure the only way to God is through Christianity. It is my preferred way and the way I hope people choose, largely due to grace; and it's the path that makes the most sense to me. I'm just not convinced it's the only way. Let me begin with this—I believe God is love. God's love is encompassing, and God loves everyone. Everyone. The Jewish mother I lived with for the summer is one of the most Christlike people I've known. I'm not convinced she is denied heaven because she came from a different religious tradition.

Between my junior and senior year of high school, I spent three months in Ghana, Africa, as a foreign exchange student. We traveled to my Ghanaian family's home village, far off the beaten path. There were children that had never seen a white person and wanted simply to touch my skin and hair. I'm not convinced an innocent child, who has had no opportunity to know Christ, will be denied heaven. When I asked my favorite theologian, my father, what he thought about other ways to God, he responded,

> I found that God is a God of love and peace in Jesus Christ for me. I take from the commission of Jesus to the disciples at the end of Matthew that we cannot save anyone. That is God's business. What God wants of his people is that we be witnesses to the world of the love and grace of God at work in our lives, and let God through the Holy Spirit take it and apply it to the hearts of others, so that their decision for Christ is a freely made one, not a forced one.

For the readers who have not thrown this book away yelling "Heretic!" or started using the pages to ignite logs in your fireplace, I hope we can agree on this: the most important thing is to live in the way of Christ and witness to grace, not to live to condemn or pronounce verdicts. We can only respond to the gift we've been given in our own life. Let's let God be God and let God determine the way to heaven.

Recognizing the need for God is a gift. Living a life after the example of Christ is a gift.

As we've moved from prevenient grace to justifying grace and now to sanctifying grace, my hope is you've come to realize that grace is a gift. Truly a gift. Because to understand grace, one *has* to see it as a gift. Recognizing the need for God and stepping into this new relationship is a gift. Living a life after the example of Christ is a gift. Bishop Kenneth L. Carder reminds us that

> grace involves both gift and response. Our identity as sons and daughters of God is God's gift to us. Living in the world as redeemed children of God is our gift to God. Justifying grace reconciles us to God, incorporates us into the body of Christ and sets us on the journey toward wholeness. Sanctifying grace continuously forms us in the likeness of Christ and sheds the love of God abroad in our hearts, our actions and our relationships. (Carder 2016)

A few years ago I was traveling and decided to attend a minor league baseball game. Paging through the program I noticed a ballplayer signed one of the ads. In the third inning it was announced that signature made me the winner of a free oil change. I picked up my certificate and gave it away to the guy sitting next to me. About the sixth inning, there was a race of mascots. Wouldn't you know it, our section won a coupon for appetizers at a local restaurant, which I proceeded to give away. In the eighth inning, a young lady came up to me and handed me an envelope and thanked me for coming to the game. I opened it up to find a coupon for dinner for two at a local restaurant. I turned to a couple behind me and asked if they lived in the area. When they said yes, I handed them the envelope and said, "Have a nice dinner." I was given three gifts in one evening and it made no sense to keep any of them. I was on my way home and had no plans to return. Of course, the people around me wanted me to become a season ticket holder and find a local apartment to rent.

It occurred to me that we need to understand that all we have is a gift from God. Our life of grace is a gift. In *Letters to an American Lady,* C. S. Lewis says: "A [person] whose hands are full of parcels can't receive a gift." How do we create space for God and to see everything as a gift? When I once told my band director that I was having trouble finding time to practice, he said, "You never have time; you need to make time." So finding space for God means making time. We are going to dive deeper into ways we can walk in grace in the next chapter, outlined in the following paragraphs.

Start with scripture. Make time to read God's Word. We become more like the creator when we understand the creator. "[You] have clothed yourselves with the new self, *which is being renewed in knowledge according to the image of its creator*" (Colossians 3:10, NRSV).

Pray more. Pray simple, earnest prayers. "And pray in the Spirit on all occasions with all kinds of prayers and requests. With this in mind, be alert and always keep on praying for all the Lord's people" (Ephesians 6:18, NIV).

Think more about God. Lately, I've been waking up singing religious songs. I think it's because I'm thinking about grace, and songs impact me. These songs are honoring God's influence on my thinking and my life. Think about Christ and create space for God. "This is what the LORD says: 'Stop at the crossroads and look around. Ask for the old, godly way, and walk in it. Travel its path, and you will find rest for your souls'" (Jeremiah 6:16, NLT).

When we accept God's grace we are saved. "Salvation is not a static, one-time event in our lives. It is the ongoing experience of God's gracious presence transforming us into whom God intends us to be" ("Our Wesleyan Heritage"). In the next chapter, we will look at means of grace or ways to live out our new life—our sanctified life, our life influenced by grace. We are going to look around, find the godly way, and walk in it. We are taking the next steps and perfecting our path of sanctifying grace.

And we pray,

Thank you for the gift of grace.
We know that you've been working on us a long time.
We ask for and give out forgiveness.
Now we move into a new stage of understanding you.

Please walk alongside us.
Please let us know you are near.
That your love and grace never fail
As we create space to know you more. Amen.

Simply Grace Story: "Rock-Bottom Days" by Greg

I was twenty-four, an alcoholic, meth addict, criminal, atheist, and probably some other negative things too harsh for this conversation. I was in Nebraska and experiencing rock bottom. It was my last winter as a slave to alcohol and drugs, and a time that I look back on now with so much love and pride (yes, my rock bottom makes me proud).

My life had sunk to the point where I had nothing; I was literally a soulless corpse. I had very few friends and those that I had weren't who you'd want as a friend. My family had completely cut me off. I had few belongings, most of which were sentimental pieces from my father, who abandoned me at the age of five. I spent my last winter in a camper shell in the northwest corner of a scrapyard. I stole from the Salvation Army drop box, after eating the food at their soup kitchen.

Now I am able to see this time as a great bookmark in my life story. I was miserable, the loneliness was overwhelming, and my thoughts were crippling. Even though I claimed to not believe in God, I recalled hundreds of times where I cried out, asking God to show me a sign, to save me, fix me, or even take me. When I didn't see the signs, I grew angrier at God. I lived this way until March 15, 1998, when I was arrested for making a couple of sales of cocaine to an "old friend," who turned out to be a confidential informant.

I'd love to tell you that while in prison I found God, but unfortunately, I did not. On September 13, 2000, at 9 a.m., Inmate #51264 walked from his cell at the Nebraska State Penitentiary to the Administration Building and was released into the free world once again. Many things had changed, but my only goal was to stay out of trouble long enough to find my old friend and seek revenge. I carried hate, anger, and contempt for most of the people I met.

About a week after I was released I started dating the woman who is now my wife. In December, we found out she was pregnant. I knew then that my life as a criminal needed to be over. I never wanted my kids to be fatherless, to feel the abandonment that my father so casually gifted to me those many years ago.

Even though I loved my firstborn child, I was by no means father material. In fact, for years I was a menace in the house. I was mentally, emotionally, financially, and sometimes even physically abusive. My two kids and older stepson were scared to death of me, and I felt like that was how a normal leader was viewed. Six years later, my wife had had enough of my "leadership" and we separated.

That summer I slept in my car at the Walmart next to where I worked. I started to sense the same feelings I had years before living in the camper shell, but this time I made a decision. I wasn't going to put my kids through this anymore, and I wasn't going down as a loser in their eyes. I knew then that my life was out of control and my family deserved a competent father. I made a call to a Christian friend I worked with who, for a couple of years, had tried desperately to introduce me to God. I started going to church with them, and for the first year, I'll be honest, I was there because I was still searching for that sign. Unfortunately, my sign came in the form of divorce papers.

That following Sunday something about the message kept me in my seat crying for long after the service. God introduced me to David, who I believe saved my life. David was part of the worship team and asked if he could hang out and pray for me, and I agreed. He prayed for what seemed like hours, and he asked God to soften my heart and my wife's heart. When he was finished praying I stood up and felt like hundreds of pounds of junk was lifted off my shoulders.

God revealed himself to me and I became a believer. I left church and immediately went to my wife's house and explained that I had met God and that I thought he would forgive me, and I asked if she would forgive me. A week later, the divorce was cancelled.

I wish I could tell you every day since then has been perfect and I never revert back to my old ways of thinking. However, what I can tell you is when my imperfections flare up, I know I have God there to save me.

The reason why I look back at my rock-bottom days with pride is that even though I claimed not to believe in God, every time I was in over my head and cried out, God was there. I didn't deserve it, but God didn't give up on me. Some might argue addiction, homelessness, anger, depression, near-death experiences, and prison sentences are not answers God would give. But I pridefully answer that God worked through these for me. When I see a homeless man, a drug addict, a convict picking up trash along the road, I am able to understand their struggle. One of my favorite songs is "Blessings" by Laura Story. My favorite phrase in the song is "What if trials of this life are your mercies in disguise?"

If you had told me twenty years ago that God would be the foundation of my life, I would have given you many reasons why I believed you were insane. On March 15, 2016, the eighteenth anniversary of my sobriety, I sent in an application for a pardon from the State of Nebraska. My application included letters from friends and family, which were all humbling. On December 1, 2016, I appeared in front of the Nebraska Board of Pardons and received notice that the State of Nebraska had approved my application for a full pardon. God answered my mess of a life with one word . . . Grace!

Since then I've become a regular visitor at the church service behind the penitentiary wall. I've even delivered a message about freedom and wealth. I'm an official volunteer with the South Dakota State Penitentiary and mentoring a young inmate.

I guess the moral to my story is this: No matter how broken you think you are, how often you sin or how ugly your sin is—God can rescue you, heal you, and use you. All God asks is that you believe in your heart that it is possible. Remember even an egg has to be broken before it can be used.

Reflection Questions

1. Can you relate to the bike ride story, where things have been going well and then a small hill or bump finds a way into your path?

2. Do you have a Holy Communion story? What have been your best Communion experiences?
3. Who are the influences on your journey toward God, in living a life of grace?
4. How would you describe grace as a gift?
5. Have you ever been so low that you didn't think you would survive?
6. Have you ever been in a situation where you couldn't get yourself out? What did you do?
7. What are some steps you can take to create space for God?

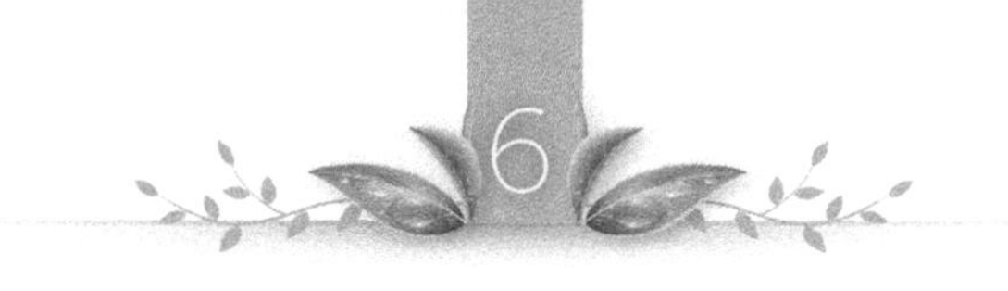

6

Means of Grace

"*The grace*-given—*give grace!*"
—Max Lucado, *Grace*

When our youngest son was in his early teens, he was in that in-between stage of work. Old enough to want to work and want money to spend, but not old enough to be hired by most businesses. So he did what a lot of other kids did at that age: he mowed yards.

One day I came home from work and noticed that the back of his friend's pickup was full of mowers, trimmers, and all kinds of lawn equipment. I asked what they were up to. The boys explained that it was more fun to mow together and it took less time if they helped each other.

That night when my son came home I inquired how this business arrangement worked.

"What do you mean?" he asked.

"Well, how does it work in terms of payment?"

"What do you mean?"

> "Well, how do you figure out how much you owe each other after mowing yards?"
>
> "You don't get it, Dad [which if you have had teenagers you are well aware this is not a new phenomenon]. We just get paid for our own yards. It goes faster to mow together, and one has a riding lawn mower that is fun to drive and another has a gas trimmer, so we just go mow yards."
>
> "Yeah, but one has much bigger yards and one of your friends gets paid more for his yards."

When I got the "Don't worry about it" and the eyes that rolled so far back into his head they almost disappeared, it hit me. I really didn't get it. I was so focused on the rules and regulations and accounting that I missed the point. They didn't care. It went faster and the work was more fun when they were together. The money was the same regardless of whether they worked alone or worked together, so why not work together?

There is so much more we can do together.

There are times in our lives that we become so focused on the rules, protocols, regulations, and what divides us that we miss the point. There is so much more we can do together.

I use this story as an introduction of living out our lives in grace. It isn't a prescribed script to live out. It isn't a list that we check off to garner favor with God. It isn't a list of good deeds versus sins and we hope the balance tips our way at the end. It isn't a list of regulations and rules to follow and then we are in the fold. God wants us to live an authentic life—not a perfect life, but an authentic life in search of God. We can do so much more together, and our life is better lived in relationship and in communion with others.

Wesley described the means of grace as channels through which God conveys grace to us. They are, as Steve Harper says, "pipelines" to find both personal and social holiness (Harper 1983). In Wesley's Sermon 16, "The Means of Grace," Wesley says, "By 'means of grace' I understand outward signs, words, or actions, ordained of God, and appointed for this end, to be the *ordinary* channels whereby he might convey to men, preventing, justifying, or sanctifying grace" (Outler and Heitzenrater 1991). In other words, we can understand God through our actions and through our steps through grace. They are ways for us to more deeply understand God and grace.

In her book *Five Means of Grace: Experience God's Love the Wesleyan Way*, Elaine A. Heath offers the simplest explanation I've found for the means of grace. She reinforces that "the acts themselves are simply channels through which grace flows." These are not meant to be "empty ritualism," where we go through the motions and check off boxes that we've completed. Rather, these are ways for God to transform our work, interaction, and grace in our everyday lives.

Heath summarizes these means of grace as:

- Prayer
- Searching the scriptures
- The Lord's Supper
- Fasting
- Christian conferencing (gathering, fellowship)

As we look at each of these means of grace, keep in mind the story of the mowers. It is not a prescribed list. Don't get caught up in looking at these as accountings of our goodness. We're in this walk together with others and with God, moving on "toward perfection" and lives filled with receiving and sending forth grace.

"Suffice it to say that prayer is the singularly central means of grace. John Wesley called it the 'chief means of grace.'"

Steve Harper, *Devotional Life in the Wesleyan Tradition*

Prayer

At the beginning of the book, I reflected about how I could feel the prayers of others in the aftermath of the earthquake in Haiti. It absolutely changed my perspective about prayer. Again, I'm not exactly sure how prayer works, but I'm convinced that prayers make a difference in us and in others. At the time of this awakening to prayer, I was working with a foundation. Often, I would write notes to donors and friends of our organization. It was not unusual for me to write that the person was in my prayers. One day it hit me—if I said the person was in my prayers, I'd made a covenant. It wasn't just a way to close a letter; it was a holy and sacred pledge that I would actually pray for the person. From that day on, I either closed a note differently or put the person on my prayer list. Because prayers have meaning and purpose and I have the responsibility to follow through.

One of the first things, and honestly one of the easiest things, to change in our spiritual walk is prayer. It's also one of the most important things—making prayer a priority so it becomes a natural, habitual part of our lives.

At first, many of us are intimidated by prayer. We don't feel that we have the right words. We feel we have to be on our knees with candles lit and an angel chorus in the background or it doesn't count. But simple, non–church words count. Long, tearful, pleading prayers count. Prayers before meals count. When we sing songs of praise, when we read scripture, when we feel close to God, and when we are thinking about God, we're praying. All earnest conversations with God count.

There are many resources on prayer. If you want an easy, practical read, try *Talking with God: What to Say When You Don't Know How to Pray* by Adam Weber. The title of the second section summarizes the best prayers: "Short. Simple. Honest." I think that says it all.

A few years ago, a good friend of mine turned me toward breath prayers. Simple prayers that last as long as a breath. When someone comes to your mind, pray for them. When someone cuts you off in traffic, pray for them (or maybe yourself first and then them). When a blessing happens in your life, praise God, or when a tragedy happens, lift it up to God with a short, simple, honest prayer.

"A little child cannot do a bad coloring; nor can a child of God do a bad prayer."

Brendan Manning, *Raggamuffin Gospel*

Searching the Scriptures

As a kid, my first Bible was a Gideon Bible. It was a King James, green-covered, tiny-print Bible full of lots of thou's and thence's. I remember thinking I needed to be disciplined and read this Bible. After the book of Genesis, it gets pretty deep. I think I made it through about the first three books and set it aside for later. Umm, maybe much later. My grandfather was a Gideon. He was a simple man with strong convictions. Grandpa would often "engage" the pastor with Grandpa's interpretation of the scripture, and sometimes at the door after the church service.

As a bit of background, Grandpa had trouble with a leg that related to an unfortunate rendezvous with a bull. Since his leg didn't work well, when we'd take his old 1950 Chevy pickup down the road, a two-by-four would be placed on the gas pedal and braced against the seat. That board served as an adapted cruise control. He'd take us on tractor rides and let us shoot his .22 rifle at pigeons in the hayloft of the barn. Grandpa was serious about most things, except for that subtle grin and huge soft spot for us grandkids.

A print of the painting *Grace*, originally a photograph by Eric Enstrom, hung over my grandparents' kitchen table. If you are not familiar with the painting, it's one of a humble elderly man, head bowed in prayer at a table, including a large Bible, bowl of soup, and loaf of bread. Minus the beard, that painting epitomizes my grandpa—a devout man who always had a Bible near. He opened every meal and many family discussions with scripture and a prayer. Grandpa lived simply and was passionate about certain things, including making sure scriptures were available to others. He worked hard, ministered in prisons up to the time of his death, and was proud to be a Gideon.

There are now so many versions of the Bible available, including what I use almost exclusively, the Bible app on my cell phone, which contains hundreds of versions. I think Grandpa would like it that people have such ready access to scripture. Now, if we'd just take advantage of that access and allow God to instruct us.

Perhaps like yours, my Bible study has been anything but methodical. I have many fits and starts into regularly reading scripture. Two things have helped me dig into scripture. The first was taking the Disciple Bible Study, a "program of disciplined Bible study aimed at developing strong Christian leaders" as described on cokesbury.com. Our disciple group met weekly; we held each other accountable for reading scripture, identifying important background and connections, writing our reflections, and discussing openly with a positive collection of Christian learners.

Another connection to scripture came through a position I held. I worked with the Dakotas United Methodist Foundation. As churches became more familiar with our ministry, I received requests to present workshops but also to preach. It forced me to dig into scripture more intently and regularly. I would borrow a volume of my dad's *William Barclay Daily Study Bible Commentaries*, and, consequently, I began to understand the importance of context and background, as well as historical and societal influences. I'm about two light-years away from being a Bible scholar, but while preparing to lead worship I began to enjoy digging into the Bible and reading multiple commentaries and explanations of scripture. That background, mixed with our own experience, helps make sense of the life of Jesus and what God intends for us. It also made me realize how the Bible challenges us in our daily lives.

If you are just starting out in a discipline of Bible study, there are tons of good resources online. Bibles comes in a variety of interpretations and versions; find the language that is comprehensible and helpful to your understanding. If you like a book in your hand, there are study Bibles that include supportive notes, maps, and other aids. My suggestion is to start in the New Testament, and many suggest reading Mark, John, Acts, and Romans first. Better yet, look for a small group or Bible study. Having the accountability of a group, along with perspectives of people who have studied the scriptures, is helpful. Just read, reflect, and realize that understanding happens in levels and the lessons deepen with time as our faith grows.

Holy Communion

My first job as principal was in a small Roman Catholic school. How a United Methodist preacher's kid became the principal of a Catholic school is a story for another day. I learned all the hand signals and still can repeat most of the prayers, but the only time I was not able to participate fully in worship was during Holy Communion, also called the Lord's Supper or Eucharist. Roman Catholics believe that the bread and wine become the physical body and blood of Christ. It is a closed Communion and available only to those within the fold who have met requirements as outlined by the church. In the United Methodist Church, on the other hand, Communion is available to young and old, and the invitation to participate is open.

Within different churches, I've seen a variety of practices. I've seen pastors use a full liturgy and pastors who basically say, "Come and get it." There is a pastor I know who has people stay after the service to eat all the bread and drink up the juice, as they believe the symbols of Christ are holy and should not just be simply discarded.

Personally, I love to see children take Holy Communion, whether or not they fully understand the symbolism. I love it when people who are on the margins with the church take Communion. To me, Holy Communion is the ultimate demonstration of grace—grace working within us and through others.

While they were eating, Jesus took bread, and when he had given thanks, he broke it and gave it to his disciples, saying, "Take and eat; this is my body." Then he took a cup, and when he had given thanks, he gave it to them, saying, "Drink from it, all of you. This is my blood of the covenant, which is poured out for many for the forgiveness of sins."

Matthew 26:26-28, NIV

Holy Communion began with Jesus and his disciples when they ate the Passover feast. Passover, as celebrated by the Jewish people, is a commemoration of their deliverance from slavery by God. By transforming with ancient ritual, Jesus created an enduring symbol of his life and ministry that cemented God's covenant, God's relationship with us through him.

A covenant signals a relationship and an enduring commitment. This bond is remembered and celebrated when we participate in Holy Communion. Through this last meal with his disciples, Jesus was saying that because of his life, death, and resurrection, we can have a new relationship with God. Or as Jesus says to Philip, "Whoever has seen me has seen the Father" (John 14:9, NRSV). By sharing this meal, Jesus showed his disciples how much God loves them in language and practices with which they were familiar. This last supper was a complete meal, not just a piece of bread and a small sip of juice. It was a meal meant to satisfy hungry people. This fact also reaches out into our everyday lives. Every time we eat and drink, we can remember God's extravagant love for us, whether it's fast food or iced tea from the convenience store. Interestingly, Quakers do not have Communion; their goal is to make every meal at every table a Lord's Supper.

Holy Communion is a mystery too deep for words. Its meaning will vary for each of us and from one time to another. But three essential meanings are caught up in this proclamation: "Christ has died; Christ is risen; Christ will come again."

Jesus gave his life so that we can be in a right relationship with God. Through Communion we acknowledge that great, undeserved gift. In so doing, we encounter God's grace. And as parts of Christ's body, we, as bread, also offer ourselves for the benefit of others and the world.

Fasting

A few years ago, I was asked to write a week of devotions for a daily devotional called *Disciplines*. I decided to spend a few days at a monastery for the first time, to help me focus on words and silence and the other ways that God speaks. Here is what I wrote.

> Recently, I spent several days at a monastery for a personal retreat. It is the monks' custom to speak little, even during meals. The first part of Psalm 19 tells us that creation itself pours forth praise for God. The heavens pour "forth speech" and declare "knowledge" of the Creator. The speaking and declaring comes without sound. When has God's creation spoken to you? What message comes through a beautiful sunrise? What do you hear in the whisper of a bird's song? What tune does the wind in the trees play for you? What does the changing moon say? What do crashing ocean waves tell us?
>
> We tend to fill the silence and stillness and wonder of God's creation with words and noise. Think about an argument that you may have had with someone or perhaps a political debate you've watched. What was the purpose of those words—to change someone's mind or straighten him or her out a bit? Someone once said that we "devour" others with our words. Our goal is to consume others and, in the end, attitudes don't change and people are angered or feel condemned. When we fill our lives with words, we also miss God's communication.
>
> Spend some time today without words, contemplating God's creation. Sense the warmth of the sunshine on your head and feel the Creator. Experience the wind blowing on your face and feel the Creator. See God's brush in the clouds and feel the Creator. Examine a unique-looking rock and feel the Creator. The messages are there; they remain unspoken. Know you are God's own design and feel the Creator. *Help us to be still, O God, and speak to us*

through your creation. Remind us that we are stewards but for a time, and we are to care for all you have created on this earth. Amen.[1]

In complete transparency, fasting has not been prominent on my list of consistent practices. I have abundant experience with eating but significantly less with denying myself food. But I use the illustration of my time at the monastery, because it is important that we seek God and look for Christ in our everyday lives. God reveals messages of grace and goodness through creation and other people if we take the time to be still and listen. Let me reiterate: the means of grace are not a checklist but disciplines to opening ourselves to the abundant love and grace of Christ.

Aaron Dragos, in his article "How John Wesley's Means of Grace Should Impact Our Christian Witness," reiterates that Wesley was quick to defend his doctrine of the means of grace against misunderstandings. He counseled Christians to remember that God is above all; there is no power in the means themselves; they do not garner favor with God; God dispenses grace; and we need to seek God alone. However, John Wesley saw fasting as integral to a Christian life. W. Paul Jones, in his paper "The Wesleyan Means of Grace," says that many of us don't practice fasting, yet this was so crucial for Wesley that when he quizzed his preachers, he didn't say, "Are you fasting?" The question was, "How do you fast every Friday?" "If" was not an acceptable question; the only one was "how." Wesley insisted that it be weekly—for health reasons, to

1 Bruce Blumer, *The Upper Room Disciplines: A Book of Daily Devotions*. Copyright 2014 by Upper Room Books. All rights reserved. Used by permission.

strengthen the will, as a liturgical (worship) act, and as an ascetic (disciplined) reenactment of our contingency before God.

Fasting as a means of grace is more than just not eating or skipping a meal here and there. The idea is that when we fast, we seek a deeper way to be mindful of who God is and how God cares for us. When we begin to feel those inevitable hunger pangs, it gives us an opportunity to redirect our focus on God. Fasting gives us a way to experience putting our self in the background and leaning on God. Naturally, when we fast we also need to be mindful of our human limitations. Food fuels our bodies and it's not good to take fasting too far. We are only human and have limits to how much we can fast. That is why fasting from food is not recommended for children and youth who are still growing or those with eating problems. But we can fast from things other than food. We can fast from gossip or watching TV or playing on our phones, for example. It's not what you fast from but that you open yourself up to God more.

In the past year, I've lost about thirty pounds. Unfortunately, some of that total has slipped back. Eating well and losing weight has been a lifelong challenge. I know what to do; I feel better when I exercise and eat well. It takes focus and discipline; it strengthens my health and my will. I guess Wesley knew that our worship of food is easier than our worship of our Lord and Savior through fasting. This is one I'm working on.

Christian Conferencing

Christian conferencing is being in fellowship and in accountability with others, and I'm learning more about this means of grace from studying the parables. As I have begun to read the parables, and read *about* parables, I've come to realize that this Jesus guy was one smart dude. He made the stories simple enough to be understood by children and profound enough to be studied for centuries by scholars. My own understanding of parables has been more like a child in front of a flannel board. But the more I learn, the more challenging parables become. It's easy to push aside the lessons and think they were just for the Pharisees and people of Jesus's time. It's hard when you realize that Jesus is talking to us today.

There is one parable in particular that reaches out to me—the parable of the weeds as found in Matthew 13:24-30 (CEB).

> Jesus told them another parable: "The kingdom of heaven is like someone who planted good seed in his field. While people were sleeping, an enemy came and planted weeds among the wheat and went away. When the stalks sprouted and bore grain, then the weeds also appeared.
>
> "The servants of the landowner came and said to him, 'Master, didn't you plant good seed in your field? Then how is it that it has weeds?'
>
> "'An enemy has done this,' he answered.
>
> "The servants said to him, 'Do you want us to go and gather them?'
>
> "But the landowner said, 'No, because if you gather the weeds, you'll pull up the wheat along with them. Let both grow side by side until the harvest. And at harvesttime I'll say to the harvesters, "First gather the weeds and tie them together in bundles to be burned. But bring the wheat into my barn."'"

J. Ellsworth Kalas, in his book *Parables from the Backside,* has an interesting take on this parable. He asks, "What is our reaction to the weeds?" Obviously, we want to get rid of them! Our world is a place where plants and weeds grow together, but what may look like a weed may just be an immature wheat plant. So, our reaction to the weeds may be setting up rules or keeping our farm small so we can control what is happening.

I wonder, what have we done in our own lives and in our churches to sow weeds into the fields? What rules have we enforced to make ourselves feel comfortable in identifying those who are weeds and those who are wheat? What have we set up that looks like we're inviting others in but in actuality serves to keep people out? When have we stayed too small and not allowed ourselves to be God-sized?

One of the greatest things I've done for my own spiritual life in the past three years is attend a men's Bible study. This has given me a new appreciation for Christian conferencing. Every member of this group is around the ages of my sons. I've learned from and appreciated this group so much, and I think they appreciate a bit of "dad wisdom" from time to time. We've had timely, honest, tough, and God-influenced discussions about our walks in the Way. Christian conferencing is being in fellowship and in accountability with others. The parable of the weeds is our inspiration to be more open and inclusive in our groups and churches. It's hard because it's uncomfortable, but Jesus implores us to include those on the fringes, those with different experiences and backgrounds in our lives. Through our experiences with these people, we grow and learn more about what it means to be the body of Christ, where there is no Jew or Greek, no male or female, as Paul teaches in Galatians 3:28.

John Wesley encouraged believers to gather in small groups or what he called "classes and bands" to "watch over one another in love." By being accountable to each other with a spirit of love, we support one another and grow in grace together, avoiding evil, doing good, and practicing the means of grace.

> One cannot be a Christian alone. What is at stake is mutual sharing for the sake of accountability, and in so being it is where sorrows are divided and joys multiplied.
>
> Paul W. Jones, *The Wesleyan Means of Grace*

I've been in a lot of churches due to my work and the positions I've held. There are warm churches and cold churches, and it has nothing to do with the size of the congregation. My observation is that many churches believe they are warm and inviting but they're not. Churches tend to be warm and inviting toward the people already on the inside and not so much to visitors or those in the early stages of checking the church out.

Not feeling welcome is just one of the reasons why people are walking away from organized religion. The statistics on "nones" is staggering. Nones are people who claim no connection to organized religion. According to Michael Lipka of the Pew Research Center, "Perhaps the most striking trend in American religion in recent years has been the *growing percentage of adults who do not identify with a religious group*. And the vast majority of these religious 'nones' (78%) say they were raised as a member of a particular religion before shedding their religious identity in adulthood."

Those of us who have been in great churches and supportive fellowship groups know their potential to impact lives. "Christian gatherings, whether in the form of public worship services or small groups, are extraordinarily powerful" (Dragos 2012). How are we sowing weeds into the wheat? How can we nurture new wheat sprouts? How can we resist keeping our farm small and comfortable? Where is God calling us to bring others into relationship with us and ultimately with God?

Wesley also talked about other ways to engage our Christian walk; they include:

1. Works of Piety (Practices That Deepen Our Faith).

    Individual Practices: reading, meditating on, and studying the scriptures; prayer; fasting; regularly attending worship; healthy living; and sharing our faith with others.

    Shared Practices: regularly sharing in the sacraments, accountability to one another, and Bible study

2. Works of Mercy (Acts of Compassion)

    Individual Practices: doing good works, visiting the sick, visiting those in prison, feeding the hungry, and giving generously to the needs of others

    Shared Practices: seeking justice, ending oppression and discrimination, and addressing the needs of the poor.

Works of mercy and works of piety are pipelines through which God conveys love and grace. They're not checklists or ways we pave our path to heaven. We can never do enough to earn our way to reach God. We don't reach God because of our "good" works. That would make our salvation depend on us, which it doesn't. God saves us because God is gracious and reaches out to us with love. Remember the boys who shared their mowing. Let's not get caught up in the rules, regulations, protocols, and what divides us. It's more fun when we work together, and there is so much more we can do together.

And we pray,

We are now living our lives out with you O Lord.
Show us clear ways, clear means to receive your grace.
We want to know you better
So we can walk lives that reflect your love.

We know that you desire for our lives and our churches to be better,
To be more accepting and open to others.
Reveal ways we can be in communion
With others not so much like us. Amen.

Simply Grace Stories: "Grace in Death"

Kandis's Story

For by grace you have been saved through faith, and this is not your own doing; it is the gift of God— not the result of works, so that no one may boast.

Ephesians 2:8-9, NRSV

Mom lived her life in faith. She was not boastful and not perfect, but I always remember her living in faith. When I was little, I spent many times going to Church Circle with my mom. The Ladies Group would meet once a month at someone's house to do a Bible Study, have coffee and cake, visit, and sometimes do a craft. Of course, the children were always welcome and we had activities to do. Before serving the coffee and cake, they would sing:

> Praise God from whom all blessings flow
> Praise him all creatures here below
> Praise him above ye heavenly hosts
> Praise Father, Son, and Holy Ghost, Amen.

I can still hear my mother's voice sing that song. Although life has taken us all a long way from that time, my mom lived in faith. About two weeks before my mother's passing, she told me she had made her peace with God. She was ready and trusted in God's grace. My mom and dad loved to play bingo. It is something they took up in their retirement to meet people and, yes, to gamble a bit. It was their entertainment, and they formed a community of friends. It was their pastime and gave them a social outing.

On February 26, 2003, my mother was placed in hospice. Her seventy-sixth birthday was to be the next day. All of her children and most of the grandchildren were coming for a birthday celebration. I was with my mom the night before the party, and we talked about how everyone was coming and that I was going to bring cake and ice cream.

Mom looked at me and said, "I am going to play bingo tomorrow." I thought to myself, *Should I bring some bingo cards so we can all play with her?* Then I said, "OK, we can do that." She told me, "No, you don't understand. I am going to be playing bingo like never before and I am going to win." I said, "OK, Mom," knowing she was on a lot of medications and painkillers. So, I said good night and told her I loved her, and I said I would see her in the morning. My brother and dad also planned to be back in the morning, and everyone else would come later in the afternoon for her birthday celebration.

On the morning of her seventy-sixth birthday, when we arrived at her room, I could sense a presence. I felt scared and sad but at the same time peaceful and calm. My mom was in a coma state. I spoke to her but she did not respond. I held her hand and made phone calls. We kept telling her we loved her and it was all going to be all right.

Mom never woke or spoke to us that day. Around 5:00 p.m., on her seventy-sixth birthday, she took her final breath and smiled at us. My mom, who always lived her life in faith, *was* playing bingo like never before.

Rev. B's Story

It was Saturday afternoon and the football game was over. I looked at the clock and decided I could make a hospital call before our evening meal. The visit was with an elderly widower named Carter, who was a gem of a person. At the last moment, I picked up my home Communion kit. The Sacrament was to be offered with the congregation on Sunday. We made small talk, and he told me he expected to go home in a day or two.

After receiving the Communion elements, we prayed the Lord's Prayer together. I heard Carter pray with me, "Our Father, who art in heaven . . ." When he came to the closing lines, Carter was not following along with me; he was praying to Jesus himself, "for thine is the kingdom, the power, and the glory, forever." He died as we were praying the Lord's Prayer. I never felt the presence of Christ more powerfully or more closely than in that moment. I was in the presence of mystery, which I do not understand, nor can I explain, nor do I want to. I am most grateful for that moment my heart and mind and soul were open to experience the presence of Christ. It was a moment of pure grace in death.

Rich's Story

My wife was starting chemo and radiation for pancreatic cancer. The doctor said that about two-thirds of the way through radiation she might end up in the hospital, as the treatment saps the body of strength. This turned out to be true.

She was not responding well in the hospital, and I thought I was going to lose her. I came home one night and got down on my knees to pray in my bedroom, laying my head on the bed, crying and praying with all my heart.

As I finished, I felt a soft touch on my head. A circle of energy surrounded my body, went down from my head to my feet, and then exited. An amazing feeling of peace washed over me for a couple of seconds. I was in awe.

As I have told this story to people, one person thought it was a hug from God. I truly believe that. My wife fought valiantly and had a relatively good life for the next three years.

Bruce's Story

My best friend went into the hospital; he had been fighting cancer for about five years. We were able to visit Rob a couple of times in the hospital before we left for a trip to San Diego. I could clearly hear Rob saying to me several times on the trip, "It will be OK."

We received a call from his daughter that things had taken a turn for the worse and Rob was not expected to make it. We were trying to make it back to say goodbye to him, but our flight was delayed in Minneapolis. While in the waiting area, I had this clear sense of peace. I looked at my watch and it was 10:25 p.m., the time I found out later they removed the ventilator.

"It will be OK" took on a completely new meaning after Rob passed away. The clear sense of peace was God showing me grace in death and allowing Rob to end his suffering.

Reflection Questions

1. Can you think of a time when you missed the "forest for the trees"? When you missed the point because you were focused on details that didn't matter?
2. Think about God and write down your prayers for one week. Do you see patterns? Who do you pray for? How has God answered your prayers? Keep a list.
3. Has the meaning of Holy Communion changed for you over time? How?
4. Is there a "means of grace" that challenges you?
5. What is your response to the Simply Grace Stories in this chapter?

What speaks to you? What challenges your faith? Where do you see God's grace?

6. If you're not already in a small group, consider starting one. Invite others to participate. Start by talking about how God is influencing your life. Use this book to talk about grace.

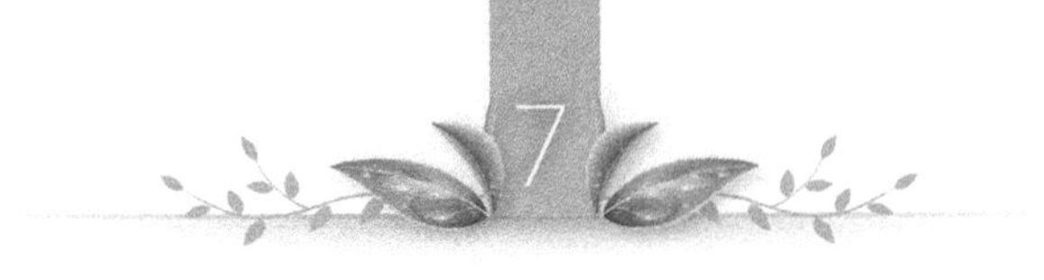

7

Cheap Grace

"The greater part of God's work in the world may go unnoticed."

–Henri Nouwen, *The Essential Henri Nouwen*

I was visiting a large city for a conference and decided to go out for a morning walk. A scruffy man was walking toward me. I forgot that I wasn't in the Dakotas and I gave him a cheery "Good morning!"

He stopped and said, "Thank you and good morning to you." I was feeling quite pleased with myself for greeting this man who appeared to be in need. But I'd only made a couple of steps farther when he said, "Sir, a minute of your time." What did I do? I switched into big-city mode and said, "Sorry" and continued my walk. I knew he wanted more than my time, and I wasn't going to give money to someone who might just use it for alcohol or something worse.

Later that day I was in the downtown area and I was walking behind a couple who had several plastic bags with Styrofoam meal holders. I thought, *My, they must be hungry to be carrying all that food.* Then God slapped me on the back of the head and said, "Pay attention." The food was not for them. It was given person by person to those along the street who were asking for money or had signs in need of food. They were ordinary people, like me, who took the time and cut through the excuses to reach out.

A speaker I heard, Molly Hough, said, "We are able to turn away from suffering. We just change the channel or page down from what we don't want to see." I have other examples where I've changed the channel or scrolled down from an opportunity to help. So how do we balance the need and ability to reach out without being suffocated by suffering? Honestly, I don't think I struggle enough with missed opportunities and turning away from opportunities to offer grace.

In our made-to-order world, do we simply form God in our image? How have we molded God to serve us? Have we made a "Country Club God"? We're so happy we're in the club. Sometimes we even make unconscious (and conscious) decisions to keep others out. We selfishly shape God to serve us.

In the book *The Case for Grace,* Lee Strobel relates the story of someone who wanted to clean up their life and who told skeptical friends he was now a Christian. The man had a relapse and then reflected, "I was only winking at God. . . . God doesn't bargain like that. Not at all. This was the cheap grace that Bonhoeffer warned about."

I love that image—winking at God. We have made the decision to follow Christ, but we look away and walk by those in need. We like the idea of being a Christian, but we don't always want to follow the example of Christ. We bargain; we pass by opportunities; we wink at God. We fall into "cheap grace."

"Cheap grace is the grace we bestow on ourselves. Cheap grace is the preaching of forgiveness without requiring repentance, baptism without church discipline, Communion without confession. . . . Cheap grace is grace without discipleship, grace without the cross, grace without Jesus Christ, living and incarnate."

Dietrich Bonhœffer, *The Cost of Discipleship*

Dietrich Bonhoeffer, a German Lutheran pastor who actively worked against Hitler, described the concept of cheap grace. The context was that pastors were preaching grace from the pulpit but keeping quiet the rest of the week, while people in their community were being abused and exterminated. After speaking out, Bonhoeffer himself was imprisoned and eventually executed by the Nazis. "Cheap grace, to Bonhoeffer, is grace that is misused. It is offered to a human being, but it does not result in a transformed life. One lives in a selfish way and it becomes cheap grace" (Holmes 2015). Philip Yancey says that cheap grace amounts to "grace abuse" (Yancy 2002).

"Our approach to the Christian life is as absurd as the enthusiastic young man who had just received his plumber's license and was taken to see the Niagara Falls. He studied it for a minute and then said, 'I think I can fix this.'"

Peter van Breemen, taken from the book
The Case for Grace by Lee Strobel

We need to be aware of the traps of cheap grace. It's about wanting forgiveness without asking God to forgive us and being unwilling to change. It's about taking steps to change the behaviors that are incompatible with Christ. It's being so emboldened that we think we have it all figured out, we don't need God, and we can fix whatever needs to be fixed, like stopping the Niagara Falls, on our own. I like what Allan Bevere says about cheap grace.

> I often compare such passive grace to going to the beach to get a suntan. We lie there on the sand doing absolutely nothing while the sun just beats down upon us giving us its light and heat, as we slowly undergo an epidermal roasting. The only thing we may do in response to our receiving the sun's "benefits" is to flip over every now and then on our back side. But God does not lavish his grace upon us so we can soak up God's forgiveness and continue to live as if it's business as usual. Divine grace is what we need from God in order to be transformed and to be re-formed after the image of God incarnated for us in Jesus Christ. God indeed accepts us as we are, but God does not intend to leave us as we are. (Bevere 2015)

Grace invites us to respond to the change in our life. We took the step to accept Christ into our lives, we asked God for forgiveness and for help to live into a new pattern of life. We respond to grace by incorporating means and channels to receive God's lessons and love. It's moving beyond a suntan God.

Here's my hunch: we've settled for wimpy grace. It politely occupies a phrase in a hymn, fits nicely on a church sign, never causes trouble or demands a response. When asked, "Do you believe in grace?" who could say no?

Max Lucado, *Grace*

I think there is another kind of cheap grace in our world: preaching the rhetoric of fear. Recently I listened to a speaker who was predicting the end times. He emphatically listed all the signs that the apocalypse is near: wars, violence, political decisions, rise in dangerous groups, lack of religious beliefs, and so on. This person has written over twenty books based on the world ending. Fear sells. Our 24/7 news cycle gives us immediate access to dangers, toils, and snares. If someone is selling fear, try to understand *their* motivation. Is it for your good or theirs?

Are there things to fear in the world? Absolutely. Every generation has had their signs of the end. Don't buy into the distress. Don't live into the rhetoric of dread. Find hope and love, ways to connect and understand others.

"So do not worry about tomorrow, for tomorrow will bring worries of its own. Today's trouble is enough for today."

Matthew 6:34, NRSV

When I was a kid I was handed a religious tract that said I was going to hell if I didn't repent. I wasn't even sure what "repent" meant, and I had recurring nightmares about a God who was going to send me to a place of eternal fire and damnation. Do we really want to promote a tract-theology God? I've come to believe in the Lamb of God and the God that shows me patience and grace and forgiveness. In my understanding, promoting fear and tract theology is cheap grace.

[The church] has been all too often guilty of preaching what Dietrich Bonhœffer called *cheap grace* and neglecting what John Wesley referred to as *perfecting grace*. We are guilty of embracing a passive grace where God dœs it all and the only response on our part is to accept it without consideration of the consequences such grace should have on our lives.

Allan Bevere, *God's Grace*

Before we all go into a funk, knowing that we haven't always kept up our end of the bargain—we don't pray enough, our Bibles are dusty, we've ignored the needs of others—we need to remember it's about grace. Perfecting grace reminds me of a school board meeting that I attended years ago. The board passed a multimillion-dollar budget without discussion but grilled the maintenance supervisor for twenty minutes about lightbulbs. I think it's because a complex, comprehensive budget isn't something we fully understand, but we can get our minds around lightbulbs. We can't fully comprehend or understand God and how God interacts with us. But we can get our minds around steps toward grace. We know the means of grace and we can change small things, common things in our lives as we move closer to grace-filled lives. As we get our minds around grace, we are more aware of the needs of others and feel called to step out and serve. We respond through the means of grace, works of piety, and works of mercy.

My wife and I started a nonprofit, La Gonave Alive, to support ministries in Haiti. La Gonave Alive supported a young Haitian man, William, to attend medical school in the Dominican Republic, and we were fortunate to be able to attend his graduation. On our first full day in the Dominican Republic, we decided to drive from Santiago to see the ocean. It's about an hour and a half drive from Santiago to the beach. We hired a driver, and William borrowed a car from a friend. While we were grateful for the use of the car, the vehicle had seen better days ten years ago.

We spent the afternoon walking the beach. Watching and listening to the waves was relaxing, but the mood changed on the way home as soon as we had a flat tire. Then we discovered that the spare tire stored in the trunk was *completely* bald, as in table-top, not-a-hint-of-tread bald. As our driver was removing the lug nuts, we found that some of the wheel studs had no thread. He rearranged the lug nuts on the remaining tires so each tire had three lug nuts that we prayed would hold. So, our trip back from the ocean was on three lug nuts and a bald tire. It made me think about how much of this world lives on three lug nuts and bald tires: the man walking the beach all day with a plastic bin, trying to sell conch meat; the young guy pushing his food cart up a big hill, looking for a good place to stop and sell to customers; the man with no foot, begging outside the food market; the woman selling beans and another woman selling beans and another selling beans, all on the same street corner; the old man delivering bananas on his bike, dodging cars and insults; the young kids sitting under a shade tree with nothing to do.

What good is it, my brothers and sisters, if someone claims to have faith but has no deeds? Can such faith save them? Suppose a brother or a sister is without clothes and daily food. If one of you says to them, "Go in peace; keep warm and well fed," but does nothing about their physical needs, what good is it? In the same way, faith by itself, if it is not accompanied by action, is dead.

James 2:14-17, NIV

When we finally made it back to Santiago, where there was a crazy amount of traffic, my wife said, "It's better to look out the side windows, so you don't have to see the mess ahead." Our lives are so comfortable. We're so insulated from other people, while across the globe people are living with three lug nuts and a bald tire. Too often we simply look out the side windows because we don't want to see the mess in front of us. God, help us to see others.

How do we pursue and receive grace? How do we not "wink" at God and fall into cheap grace? These questions may be answered in one of the simplest and most profound books to summarize Wesley's teachings and guide our response, *Three Simple Rules* by Reuben Job. The rules are:

1. Do no harm—Be on guard not to harm any of God's children or God's creation.
2. Do good—Do good whenever and wherever we can.
3. Stay in love with God—Pray, read scripture, participate in community, participate in Holy Communion and other disciplines to stay connected and grow in love of God.

We walk away from cheap grace and walk into true grace, to become more authentic, and simply say to God, "I come just as I am."

And we pray,

Give us eyes to see
And provide us with opportunities to serve.
Help us to understand the needs of others
And to make a difference where we are able.

We are thankful for your grace
But know that grace takes a response and action.
Thank you for accepting us as we are
But not leaving us as we are. Amen.

Simply Grace Story: "Deep Waters" by Sharilyn

Recently, I read a devotion by Priscilla Shirer where she talked about Mary at the time of the birth of Jesus. She referred to the verse in Luke 2 that tells us, "Mary treasured up all these things and pondered them in her heart" (v. 19, NIV). Priscilla's devotion is an encouragement to treasure the times in our own lives where we experience God and to recognize the great value in our personal interaction with God. To hold those moments in our hearts and memories as a great treasure. Through God's mercy and grace, the difficult journey of my daughter's illness and death is a memory that I have grown to treasure. Jennifer's story is not just about her life's journey, but about God's story within her life's story.

Jennifer was my first baby who made me a mom for life. From the start, she was outgoing, energetic, strong-willed, and fun, and she passionately filled her role of big sister to her three younger siblings. Jen was responsible, outspoken, loyal, and always available to her family and friends. She was always a good student and was involved in both church and school activities.

We attended a church where, as a believer, you would publicly profess your faith to the church when you made the decision to accept Jesus as your Savior. Jen made her profession of faith in January 1995. We celebrated the occasion with her, and I gave her a card that included the Philippians 1:6 verse, which reads, "Being confident of this, that he who began a good work in you will carry it on to completion until the day of Christ Jesus" (NIV). Strangely, that verse always stuck with me in memory of that day and became the verse I prayed over Jen's life and the lives of my other three kids.

Jennifer loved special-needs children and spent her career focused on developing and supporting them and their families, and she mostly focused on children with autism. Most weekends, she also worked at the Ronald McDonald Family Room in a children's hospital.

During one Christmas at our house, Jen announced that she wanted to learn to knit and that I would be learning along with her. Off we went to the local yarn shop to grab some yarn, needles, and a "learn to knit" book to begin our knitting hobby. She learned everything from that "learn to knit" book and YouTube videos. Soon *everybody* in the family and all her friends had a knit hat and pair of socks, so she had to move on to a new knitting project. Because of her love for babies, booties and baby hats were her natural next project. Since her family and friends couldn't provide her with enough babies fast enough, she needed an outlet for her accumulating knitting projects. So, she opened an online shop on Etsy where she could sell her knitting creations!

We were good friends, but I was always mom to her. She called me every day—most often two to three times a day. She was continuing to find her way through life and her faith, and there were often growing pains. So I walked through both the joy and the muck with her.

In early October 2014, Jennifer spent a week in Mexico to be a bridesmaid in her friend's wedding. On the day she was flying home she mentioned that she was not feeling well. She had stomach cramps, was tired, and felt pretty much "blah." We both agreed she most likely ate something that caused the typical stomach issues after traveling to Mexico and thought it would most likely go away in a few days. Unfortunately, that was not the case. She continued to feel worse—very fatigued and weak, with loss of appetite and continued stomach, digestive issues.

By Halloween, she began noticing jaundice, as her eyes and skin appeared yellow. As her symptoms and jaundice continued to worsen, she was sent to a liver specialist at the University of Minnesota hospital. The tests there were inconclusive, but her condition progressed to where she could no longer work full days and started doing some work from home.

I was looking forward to seeing her and taking care of her when she came to our house for Thanksgiving—hoping that by then she would be on the upswing and feeling better and believing mom's care, food, and rest would make a difference! When I got home from work one day, I was distraught at how weak, sick, and yellow she was. I took her to the emergency room and they almost immediately decided to send her by ambulance to the larger University of Iowa hospital.

Despite numerous tests and consultations and specialists, the condition was unresolved; they suggested a liver biopsy. At that point, Jen wanted to go back to Minneapolis to her home and doctors and have the biopsy done there. In Minneapolis, we were unexpectedly and shockingly told that she would need a liver transplant. There is a ranking scale to determine who receives priority for available livers, and they said Jen would be assigned a high ranking for immediate need due to the seriousness of her condition. And just that quickly, we took a deep plunge into some scary waters!

There were a flurry of tests and consultations, but finally an identification was completed. Jen was given a diagnosis of HLH. I'm not even going to attempt to tell you what the acronym stands for, but it is an extremely rare, life-threatening blood disease, which is actually more often seen in babies and young children. HLH is an autoimmune blood disorder where the white blood cells attack the red blood cells and organs. The doctors had seen HLH previously, but rarely, and never with liver failure to this extent. It was a unique, complicated case with no typical diagnosis. We don't know, and may never know, what triggered HLH in her body, but it is what caused her liver to fail so quickly, which then adversely affected other body functions. So now that we had some answers, the battle began to fight it and get her strong enough for transplant surgery.

I was with Jen the entire time in the hospital, but then family showed up. I was never more impressed with my kids than to watch them calmly care for and fight for their big sister through extremely tense, overwhelming, and scary situations and conversations. They were brave and strong. They were wise. They were all defenders, protectors, and advocates for Jen. We were sustained by the constant prayers of so many, and God's presence and peace covered all of us.

While Jen lay in her hospital bed, I often whispered in her ear: "Just stick with Jesus. Just stay with him. He'll walk you through this." But after a while, my whispered encouragement to her was instead, "Just let Jesus carry you. He's going to carry you through." One of the nights when I was staying overnight in the room with Jen, I had a picture in my mind of our experience. I was no longer above the water, but instead I pictured the tall, robed figure of Jesus carrying Jen across the floor of an ocean valley while the rest of our family huddled close to him as we followed him across the valley. Let Jesus carry you, Jen.

On Friday, December 12, at the age of thirty-four, Jennifer Jean took her last breath on this earth surrounded by the love and presence of her family. There was a most unexplainable peace about all of it. God's presence and peace was so real to us. It filled the room, covered our family, and strengthened our hearts. Tears flowed, but quiet tears. There was a confidence in knowing it was Jennifer's time to go and there were no frantic, grasping fears in letting her go. It was a beautiful experience and an amazing gift for our family. A few weeks later I had the most amazing realization that I had been blessed to be present at both my daughter's very first breath on this earth and her last.

On the drive, I also wondered how my first night at home was going to go. I couldn't imagine that I would sleep at all. I actually fell asleep right away, but I woke up sometime in the middle of the night. I knew I was in my own bedroom and in my own bed, but I remember thinking, *Where am I?* I was curled up in a pure white—nest? *Nest* is the word that came to my mind. But a nest of what? Are they white feathers? No. A soft, fluffy cotton? No. It was so real but something I couldn't describe. I remember thinking, *I don't know what it is, but I don't care. I like it. I feel safe, warm, and secure.* So I curled up in my pure white nest, went back to sleep, and slept peacefully until morning. I feel in my heart that I was sleeping in God's arms that night, and God had graciously given me just a glimpse of what that was like.

That next morning I got up and grabbed my Bible to do my morning devotions. I got on my knees and laid it open in front of me on the living room floor. I had no idea what I was going to say to my God that morning. But words poured out of me: "Thank you! Thank you! Thank you for coming through for Jen." I clearly remember thinking, *Ugghh. Where are these words coming from? I just lost my daughter and all that flows out of my mouth are words of praise and thanks?* It was God's assurance to me that God was in control and that all was well. I found encouragement in the Spirit's words that came through me that morning.

I am still at a loss for words to describe what it has felt like to lose Jennifer. I have often said I live in an unreal reality of living out my life with one of my children gone before me. It's not just sadness and a feeling of loss, but I've experienced a deep grief, an unfillable, unique absence, and a pain in my chest that physically cuts into my heart and breath. When I try to describe it even to myself, I have found myself considering words that just simply fall short of the emotion, the ache, the loss, the hole that is left inside me and our family. I have basically given up trying to find the right words.

However, words like *peace, grace, love, hope,* and *eternity* are richly fulfilling to me now. They have a deeper meaning now than I ever felt or understood before, and I literally drink them in. These words describe the work that God has done to bring Jen home and to fill the hole and ease the ache since she's been gone. Through Jennifer's illness, hospitalization, and death, I've personally experienced his words of Psalm 18:16 to be true: "He reached down from on high and took hold of me; he drew me out of deep waters" (NIV).

I have discovered another truth that I may have only learned through trusting God in the deep waters. I learned to trust by leaving the comfort of the shore and in meeting God out in the unknown, in the scary, deep waters. When I was at my most vulnerable, my most raw and naked, my most helpless—that was when I was truly able to know God, to learn to trust him and to fully experience his power, his love, his faithfulness, and his grace.

My desire is to live a life of faith and trust—both in the joys and in the struggles of this life. I pray that the next time Jesus calls me out onto the waters that he would give me the courage to leave the comfort of the shore and once again meet him there in the unknown where I can trust him with the outcome and my faith can grow. I now know that we can trust that God is already there, well ahead of us.

Reflection Questions

1. Have you missed opportunities to help others? What could you do the next time?
2. Where have you seen grace abuse in your life or the lives of others?

3. What do you fear? What may be the root of these fears?
4. Name one thing that might be cheap grace in your life.
5. Where do you see people living on "three lug nuts and a bald tire"? How can you involve your friends, church, small group, or family in helping?
6. Why might it be so difficult to reach out to God when you've suffered tragedy?
7. Why do some people grow closer to God in times of trouble and others push God away?

Faith and Forgiveness

"Faith is taking the first step, even when you don't see the whole staircase."

—Martin Luther King Jr.

Faith

I was too young at the time to remember all the details, but when I was a child Dad invited an atheist to speak during a worship service, a pretty gutsy move for the pastor of a church in a small town in the Dakotas in the 1960s. It attracted newspaper coverage and I know it attracted harsh criticism.

Recently, I asked Dad why he invited an atheist to speak and what happened afterward. Dad said he was doing a series on difficult issues in the church. He said actually the congregation members were mostly supportive. They looked on it as a perspective and a way to sort out the issues important to their own faith. However, a church in another state put together a petition to revoke my father's clergy credentials because of it, and Dad said he probably wouldn't do something as controversial again.

Isn't it a shame that we're afraid to confront questions about our faith? Isn't it a shame that churches fear taking on difficult conversations in a spirit of learning? One of the members of Dad's congregation said after the fallout, "If we can't handle a couple of atheists in our own den, how weak is *our* faith?" I couldn't agree more.

In an earlier chapter, I confessed my spiritual gift of doubt. I also outlined how my Christian faith was solidified by living with a Jewish family. I'm OK if you doubt. People come to faith through doubt. Doubt can serve as a tool to help chip away the superstition, the nonessentials, the things that cloud our view. Yes, doubt is a spiritual gift from God. But my fear is for those who don't seek out others to help them navigate through their doubt. The statistics indicate that people are moving away from organized religion. Michael Shermer estimates that 64 million Americans—approximately 26 percent of the population—are athiest. Further, 27 percent report being "spiritual but not religious" (Shermer 2018). I do think we need to examine the ways our churches and we as individuals can be more invitational, more welcoming, more grace-filled, because as psychologists have known a long time, we typically see people less like who they are and more like who we are.

One of the ways I believe we open the doors to our hearts and the doors of our churches is through grace—not to use God's words as weapons against others, not to promote "conversion by concussion" (Manning 2005). But to "preach the gospel at all times, and if necessary use words" (attributed to St. Francis of Assisi).

When others see grace in us, they
see God. When they see God, they

want to seek God. When they seek God, they grow in God's grace. This is the cycle of grace or "grace upon grace," as John Wesley would say.

This year we had a particularly long winter, deep snow when we should have had green grass and flowers. These brutal days in the wrong season made me think about the years that I delivered newspapers. Delivery day started early, when I counted out the newspapers, then loaded the bags and strapped them across both shoulders. Even though it was many years ago, I can see the path and the houses where I delivered papers. While there were beautiful mornings, it is easier to remember the cold and the wind—in the Dakotas, always wind. In the dead of winter and about halfway through my route, I'd turn back, to the west. That's when the icy winds pinched my skin, the bags began to dig deeper into my shoulders, and the steps became more plodding. As newspapers continued to be delivered, the bags got lighter, the promise of warmth and breakfast came closer, and much like horses returning to their barn, my pace quickened.

People I have known who have impressed me with their faith, regardless of age, have gone through some cold, blustery days. They have faced the wind without relenting. They have plodded and not given up. Along the way, they have learned to dump some of their baggage. Their daily steps lead to deeper trust, hope, and promise, which lifts the head and quickens the pace.

Trust, and the load will become lighter. Hope, and the steps become easier. Believe, and the promise is fulfilled, through faith.

Forgiveness

Our family experienced a church leader who misused their position. It led to one of our children being put in a difficult situation, one that should never have been allowed to happen. Because the leader was able to control the narrative, it put us at odds with others and the leader wasn't, in our opinion, held accountable. This led to anger and resentment.

Sometime later, a friend contacted me and said I had opened their eyes to their own resentment. They had been carrying bitterness too long and explained how they were working on letting it go. In making *them* aware, it struck me that *I* was carrying hefty resentment about things I can't change, things that are in the past, things I need to let go of, things for which I need to forgive. Often when you are talking to others you are really saying what *you* need to hear. The struggle for me is between forgiveness and forgetting and the resentment that can result. These words from M. L. Stedman provide guidance for me: "You only have to forgive once. To resent, you have to do it all day, every day. You have to keep remembering all the bad things" (Stedman 2012).

"Forgiveness is not just an occasional act: it is a permanent attitude."

Martin Luther King Jr.

I think we can learn much from those who have forgiven. Really forgiven. The book *Amish Grace* describes the horrific event of a young man who held hostages in a one-room Amish schoolhouse. The shooter let some of the students go but killed five children and then himself. The family of one of the girls who was killed went to the family of the shooter to forgive, and they actually attended the funeral of the shooter. As the author of *Amish Grace*, Donald Kraybill, says: "Forgiveness is woven into the fabric of Amish faith. And that is why words of forgiveness were sent to the killer's family before the blood had dried on the schoolhouse floor. It was just the natural thing to do, the Amish way of doing things. Such courage to forgive has jolted the watching world as much as the killing itself" (Kraybill 2007).

I was able to hear Immaculee Ilibagiza, a survivor of the Rwandan genocide, speak and read from her book *Left to Tell*. Due to tribal tensions and the president's plane being shot down, a killing spree began, which targeted the Tutsi people. During the bloodshed, Immaculee and seven other women hid in a small bathroom for three months and she lost nearly fifty pounds during this ordeal. When Immaculee was finally able to leave the hiding place, she learned that her entire family had been murdered. Immaculee chose to forgive the people who killed her family because she knew the bitter feelings and rage were destroying her. Though not easy, she was determined to let forgiveness, rather than hate, rule her life. Eventually, she met with one of the murderers face-to-face and told him directly that she forgave him.

Another example of extreme forgiveness comes from the Truth and Reconciliation Commission (TRC), which was established by the South African government with the support of some churches, to bring healing and reconciliation by uncovering the human rights violations that had occurred under apartheid (rule by the white minority and enforced segregation). The focus of the TRC is uncovering and sharing information and not on prosecuting individuals for past crimes, seeking to heal victims and victims' families. The commission held public hearings and heard more than twenty-two thousand statements from victims. Not only did victims give testimony but so did the perpetrators who were allowed to openly confess and seek forgiveness from their victims. These testimonies were not easy to hear; they included torture, murder, kidnapping, rape—a litany of the worst crimes humans can do to each other. Some people confessed things that they had done in secret. Others confessed things they had done openly, with the full knowledge of the government. Some of the perpetrators were white; some were black. The TRC was an experiment of sorts, and many people held their breath, fearing a backlash of reprisals and more violence. Surprisingly, forgiveness was offered and accepted, and healing began in earnest for the victims, perpetrators, and nation. In addition, the TRC has become a model of reconciliation for other conflicts across the world. Later the new president, Desmond Tutu, said,

> When I talk of forgiveness I mean the belief that you can come out the other side a better person. A better person than the one being consumed by anger and hatred. Remaining in that state locks you in a state of victimhood, making you almost dependent on the perpetrator. If you can find it in yourself to forgive then you are no longer chained to the perpetrator. You can move on, and you can even help the perpetrator to become a better person too. (The Forgiveness Project)

Not long ago, journalists interviewed families involved in yet another tragic school shooting. Understandably, some families were angry and wanted to inflict pain and seek revenge. But one parent said the only way to move on was to forgive—and this parent made contact with the shooter's family. Forgiveness for something of this magnitude does not come easy or fast. It takes time to grieve the wound, the suffering. Forgiveness does not take suffering away, but it is part of the healing process. And we know from our own cuts and bruises, healing takes time—and sometimes a lifetime; and sometimes healing only comes in the life beyond death.

The biblical word for healing is *shalom*, which literally means "knitting of the bones." We often hear the word *shalom* as a synonym for "peace." And it is, but it's also much more. Shalom means healing, peace, and wholeness. The Bible also makes it clear that shalom is a gift from God. It is a manifestation of God's grace.

And the peace [shalom] of God, which surpasses all understanding, will guard your hearts and your minds in Christ Jesus.

Philippians 4:7, NRSV

But when we fill our lives with resentment, we aren't able to receive God's shalom. Resentment closes us off from the good God has for us and, in the end, resentment walls us off from God altogether. That is why forgiveness is so important. It's a way we extend God's grace, and, in so doing, we can deepen our relationship with God. Faith and forgiveness are integral elements to our journey. Both involve trust and belief in the midst of doubt and uncertainty. Both involve mountain peaks and deep valleys, but each is core to moving toward perfection, toward the life and light of Christ.

The Bible says we are as lumps of clay molded by our Maker, the Master Potter. As mentioned earlier in this book, I like to also believe that we begin as dough that is lovingly kneaded and shaped by God's prevenient grace even before we're aware. Through God's grace we can accept God and enter into an intentional relationship. We may be lured, prodded, and nudged by God, but once we accept God's invitation to enter in through God's justifying grace, we are different. We begin to explore God's "house" and actively seek to share the love of God with others in more and more significant ways through sanctifying grace. And like Christ, who is the Bread of Life, we become bread for others as we commune and serve them, as we walk toward godliness, as we become Holy Communion, allowing God to live in us and others. It's simply grace. My deepest prayer is that we see it's simply grace in our everyday glimpses of God.

Simply Grace Story: "Giving Up Control" by Jerry

While I was raised in a Christian home and even attended a Catholic elementary school, I had no real relationship with God. In high school I started drinking, mostly just to fit in with the cool crowd. In college, my partying and drinking only increased. Balancing school, jobs, and sports seemed easy. Even with my bad habits and poor decisions, my drinking still hadn't landed me in any real trouble. But by the time I was twenty-two years old, I had accumulated a few alcohol-related misdemeanors, minor consumptions, disturbing the peace, open container, and a Driving Under the Influence (DUI). Still I felt like this was normal and that I was in control. After all, I had a good life and was building a good career.

When I was twenty-eight years old, I was pulled over for my second DUI in a company vehicle on my way home from a work-related event. All of a sudden, my lifestyle and bad choices had created real trouble. I could lose my job; I could lose my fiancée; and a third DUI would be a felony. I felt like I could lose all that I had worked for, and suddenly I was no longer in control. Luckily, the judge who sentenced me required that I complete an outpatient alcohol treatment program.

The counselor I was working with made it clear to me that normal people don't get a second DUI unless they have a problem with control. My work life has been in the area of construction, where control is a major part of the job. Looking back, I could see my need for control was also a major part of my relationships.

One of the twelve steps is that God is in control and can restore us. I felt it in my heart that I needed to let go and reconnect with my faith. It made me realize how far I had drifted and how close I came to throwing so much away. It helped me begin to understand that *God* is in control.

The layers started falling away; I began to see how selfish I was, and I began letting go of the control I thought I had, and let God lead the way. My fiancée and I started going to church and it felt like home. The pastor's sermons seemed like they were designed for us, that he was speaking directly into our lives.

The next pastor appointed to this same church further

challenged my faith. I've always been into leadership and self-help books, but this pastor also turned me toward the Bible. Through Bible study and the book *The Purpose Driven Life* by Rick Warren, I began to understand the importance of my personal mission. It made me focus on being a better father, husband, leader, and follower of Christ. It clarified for me who I am and why I am here.

Working my way through the ranks of a major construction company, I not only understand everyone's role but now believe in using my platform to grow others and to be in service to others. I like to make sure our workers connect to the bigger mission, that their labor is important and the hospital or school or place of business they are building will be a place that assists others and the greater good.

Another discipline that I have learned that has helped me greatly is taking time for daily reflection. I've tried a few different times of day, but the mornings work best for me. I keep a daily prayer journal and seek stillness, clarity, and focus before the busyness of life and the job takes over.

I can't express how important it has been to have my wife in my faith journey. We encourage and challenge each other. Our first child was born ten weeks early and I was challenged by the difficulties and risks. Through this demanding time, we grew together, and it was a big stepping-stone for our faith and marriage.

Letting go and letting God also led to some big decisions. We decided to have my wife stay home with our three kids and to begin tithing to the church. Money was tight, and it was a stressful decision, but we gave up our control to God.

There was a time that we prayed together about a job

opportunity. We now see that God gave us the patience to wait. That time of waiting led to some issues being resolved and ultimately to a lead role that has allowed me to stay and help grow a vital construction company.

My faith journey also pushes me to set priorities. I set an alarm on my phone for 5:00 p.m. that it's time to go home. Another alarm at 5:14 p.m. that my life is getting away from me. It helps me realize I have another important role and my family needs me. As I head home, I remember to accept and be thankful for all the blessings on the other side of the front door of my house.

Conclusion

What is simply grace? It is kindness given in return for sorrow; it's seeing the good in others while also recognizing their limitations; it's goodwill for our neighbors, our coworkers, our children, our parents, and the prodigals who return; it's offering second chances even as we are wise as serpents and gentle as doves; it's offering empathy even when it's hard to listen; it's giving a cup of cold water and dinner to those without.

What might grace involve? Telling inconvenient truth in love to the boss, our best friend; serving the needs of outsiders when others refuse; helping someone who feels entitled who has no right to expect it; loving those who only God can love.

Grace is the firm foundation of any loving family, the source of respect in the workplace, the basis of any successful marriage. As ordinary people, even in our selfishness, we long for grace from others and we long for grace from God. We know we are undeserving; we know we can't earn it or even pay it back, but we ask and know God's grace will not disappoint.

And we pray,

Reassure us, O Lord, in our times of doubt.
Give us the confidence of your love.
Turn our times of unbelief
Into faith that endures and strengthens.

Help us to provide and receive forgiveness,
To understand your love through acceptance,
To let go of resentments and pain,
Knowing they don't serve us and don't allow us to serve you. Amen.

Reflection Questions

1. When has your faith been the strongest? When has doubt dominated your thoughts? How can doubt help you deepen your faith?
2. What and who helps grow your faith and connection to God?
3. Who are people you know that have strong faith? What can we learn from them? How have they handled misfortune and being mistreated?
4. Where do you see examples of forgiveness? Share a time when you or someone you knew offered forgiveness.
5. Are there people you need to forgive? Are there people who need to forgive you?
6. Have you ever come close to "throwing it all away"? What happened?

7. List resentments and anger you currently carry. Give it to God and let them go.
8. What are your next steps in your relationship with God? How can you open yourself up to seeing God's grace in your everyday life?

Bibliography

Bevere, Allan R. "God's Grace Is Not Equivalent to Getting a Suntan." October 26, 2015. MinistryMatters.com.

Bonhoeffer, Dietrich. *The Cost of Discipleship.* New York, NY: Touchstone, 1995.

Bridges, Jerry. *The Discipline of Grace: God's Role and Our Role in the Pursuit of Holiness.* Colorado Springs, CO: NavPress, 2006.

Carder, Kenneth. "A Wesleyan Understanding of Grace." *Interpreter,* November–December 2016.

Disciple I Becoming Disciples Through Bible Study: Study Manual. 2nd ed. Nashville, TN: Abingdon Press, 2003.

Disciplines 2014. Nashville, TN: Upper Room Books, 2013.

"Distinctive Wesleyan Doctrines." First United Methodist Church Wichita Falls, Wichita Falls, TX. www.fumcwf.org/wesleyan-doctrines.

Dragos, Andrew. "How John Wesley's Means of Grace Should Impact Our Christian Witness." Seedbed.com. May 29, 2012. https://www.seedbed.com/how-john-wesleys-means-of-grace-should-impact-our-christian-witness/.

Harper, Steve. *Devotional Life in the Wesleyan Tradition.* Nashville, TN: Upper Room Books, 1983.

Haynes, Donald. "Taking Methodist Fundamentals into the Future." *United Methodist Reporter,* March 18, 2011.

Haynes, Donald. "Wesleyan Wisdom: Methodist Fundamentals Draws Heavy Reader Response." May 28, 2011. www.UMPortal.org.

Heath, Elaine A. *Five Means of Grace: Experience God's Love the Wesleyan Way.* Nashville, TN: Abingdon Press, 2017.

Holmes, Cecile S. *Wesleyan Way* (blog), October 26, 2015. http://www.interpretermagazine.org/topics/the-gift-of-grace.

Ilibagiza, Immaculee. *Left to Tell: Discovering God Amidst the Rwandan Holocaust.* Carlsbad, CA: Hay House, 2014.

Job, Reuben. *Three Simple Rules.* Nashville, TN: Abingdon Press, 2007.

Jones, Paul W. "The Wesleyan Means of Grace." In *Wesleyan Spirituality in Contemporary Theological Education: Report of a Consultation.* Nashville, TN: GBHEM, 1982.

Kalas, J. Ellsworth. *Parables from the Backside.* Nashville, TN: Abingdon Press, 1998.

Kraybill, Donald B. *Amish Grace*. San Francisco, CA: Jossey-Bass, 2007.

Lewis, C. S. *Letters to an American Lady.* Grand Rapids, MI: Eerdmans, 1950; reissue edition, 2014.

Lipka, Michael. "Why America's 'Nones' Left Religion Behind." https://www.theaquilareport.com/why-americas-nones-left-religion-behind/.

Lucado, Max. *Grace: More Than We Deserve, Greater Than We Can Imagine*. Nashville, TN: Thomas Nelson, 2014.

Maddox, Randy. *Responsible Grace: John Wesley's Practical Theology.* Nashville, TN: Kingswood Books, 1994.

Manning, Brendan. *The Ragamuffin Gospel*. Sisters, OR: Multnomah, 2005.

"Our Wesleyan Heritage." The United Methodist Church. http://www.umc.org/what-we-believe/our-wesleyan-heritage.

Outler, Albert C., and Richard P. Heitzenrater, eds. *John Wesley's Sermons: An Anthology.* Nashville, TN: Abingdon Press, 1991.

Shermer, Michael. "Silent No More." *Scientific American* (April 2018): 77.

Spurgeon, Charles. *All of Grace.* Chicago, IL: Moody Publishers, 1974.

Stedman, M. L. *The Light Between the Oceans.* New York, NY: Scribner, 2012.

"Stories." The Forgiveness Project. www.theforgivenessproject.com/stories/desmond-tutu-south-africa.

Strobel, Lee. *The Case for Grace.* Grand Rapids, MI: Zondervan, 2015.

Tietz, Christiane. *Theologian of Resistance: The Life and Thought of Dietrich Bonhoeffer.* Minneapolis, MN: Fortress Press, 2016.

United Methodist Hymnal. Nashville, TN: Abingdon Press, 1989.

Weber, Adam. *Talking with God: What to Say When You Don't Know How to Pray.* Colorado Springs, CO: WaterBrook, 2017.

"Welcome to First Friends Church." Whittier First Friends Church: A Quaker Meeting. www.firstfriendswhittier.org/welcome/sacraments.html.

Wesley, John. *The Principles of a Methodist Farther Explained*. Vol. 9 of *The Works of John Wesley*, edited by Rupert E. Davies. Bicentennial Edition. Nashville, TN: Abingdon Press, 1989.

"The Wesleyan Means of Grace." The United Methodist Church. http://www.umc.org/how-we-serve/the-wesleyan-means-of-grace.

Yaconelli, Michael. *Messy Spirituality: God's Annoying Love for Imperfect People*. Grand Rapids, MI: Zondervan, 2013.

Yancey, Philip. *What's So Amazing About Grace*. Grand Rapids, MI: Zondervan, 2002.

CPSIA information can be obtained
at www.ICGtesting.com
Printed in the USA
FFHW022137060619
52852162-58404FF

9 781945 935381